D1300477

Uncomplicating
FRACTIONS
to Meet Common Core
Standards in Math, K–7

372.72
Sm181

Uncomplicating
FRACTIONS
to Meet Common Core
Standards in Math, K–7

MARIAN SMALL

Nyack College - Bailey Library
One South Blvd.
Nyack, NY 10960

TEACHERS COLLEGE PRESS

Teachers College, Columbia University
New York and London

NATIONAL COUNCIL OF
NCTM TEACHERS OF MATHEMATICS
1906 Association Drive, Reston, VA 20191
www.nctm.org

NELSON EDUCATION

www.nelson.com

Published simultaneously by Teachers College Press, 1234 Amsterdam Avenue, New York, NY 10027, and National Council of Teachers of Mathematics, 1906 Association Drive, Reston, VA 20191; distributed in Canada by Nelson Education, 1120 Birchmount Road, Toronto, ON, Canada M1K 5G4.

Copyright © 2014 by Teachers College, Columbia University

All rights reserved. No part of this publication may be reproduced or transmitted in any form or by any means, electronic or mechanical, including photocopy, or any information storage and retrieval system, without permission from the publisher.

Text Design: Lynne Frost

Library of Congress Cataloging-in-Publication Data

Small, Marian, author.
   Uncomplicating fractions to meet common core standards in math, K–7 /
   Marian Small.
      pages   cm
   Includes bibliographical references and index.
   ISBN 978-0-8077-5485-6 (pbk. : alk. paper)
   ISBN 978-0-8077-7303-1 (ebook)
      1. Fractions—Study and teaching (Elementary)   I. Title.
   QA137.S64 2014
   372.7'2—dc23   2013030771

ISBN 978-0-8077-5485-6 (paper)
eISBN 978-0-8077-7303-1
NCTM Stock Number: 14817

Printed on acid-free paper
Manufactured in the United States of America

21 20 19 18 17 16 15 14   8 7 6 5 4 3 2 1

CONTENTS

PREFACE

ORGANIZATION OF THE BOOK

The title of this resource includes the word *Uncomplicating*. The choice of that term is based on the premise that the way we uncomplicate what we teach is not to come up with a formulaic approach to instruction but to provide the opportunity for a deep and rich understanding of what is being learned. Many teachers have described to me the difficulty their students experience in learning about fractions. Therefore, it seemed valuable to try to "uncomplicate" that particular topic.

This resource is organized by grade level around the Common Core State Standards for Mathematics (CCSSM) related to fractions and to some extent to decimals, ratios, and proportional thinking. The grades covered in this resource begin with Grade 1, where the first relevant standard is found in the geometry domain, and end with Grade 7, where the focus is on operations with rational numbers and proportional thinking. In each case, a portion of the relevant standard is presented, followed by a delineation of important underlying ideas associated with that portion of the standard, as well as some good questions to ask to bring out those underlying ideas.

Those underlying ideas include:

* background to the mathematics of the standard
* suggestions for appropriate representations, including manipulatives, for those specific mathematical ideas
* suggestions for explaining ideas to students, and
* cautions about misconceptions or situations to avoid

Following each set of underlying ideas is a group of questions that can be used for either classroom instruction, practice, or assessment. These include many open questions, as well as more directed conceptual, rather than procedural, questions that might be supplemental to what teachers are normally provided in the resources they use. In addition, specific mention is often made of the Common Core State Standards for Mathematical Practice.

For Whom Is This Book Useful and Why?

This resource is designed to aid math teachers of Grades 1–7 to help students become more proficient and more comfortable working with situations involving fractions. It is also planned as a resource for math coaches in assisting classroom teachers in their transition to teaching mathematics within the demanding framework of the Common Core State Standards. These new standards challenge all of us to help students become mathematical thinkers, not just mathematical "doers"; the goal has become the development of students who can reason and represent mathematical situations in multiple ways, and explain their reasoning to others. I also expect this book to be helpful to preservice teachers as they prepare themselves to understand and teach math to foster a deep level of understanding.

Considering the Bigger Picture

While I hope that all readers will read the entire book, I particularly suggest this approach for math coaches and preservice teachers. For grade-level or grade-band teachers, I suggest reading the Introduction and the grade-level sections that most directly apply for their particular groups of students, but also becoming acquainted with the mathematics related to fractions taught in grades directly below and above. Because students in any classroom are at different levels of knowledge, in order to differentiate instruction appropriately, the teacher must be aware of missing prerequisite knowledge as well as suitable directions for moving forward.

Lastly I hope that reading this book ensures that math makes more sense both to the readers and, ultimately, to their students.

ACKNOWLEDGMENTS

I have been fortunate to work with excellent editors with Teachers College Press, and I would like to thank them for both their faith in me and their support.

I have also had the good fortune to have met so many teachers who have responded positively to my approach to mathematics teaching and learning. They have continued to encourage me to write more. I would like to thank these professionals for their personal support, as well as for sharing my work with colleagues.

I would also like to thank the reviewers who looked at earlier versions of this manuscript and who made very helpful comments.

Uncomplicating
FRACTIONS
to Meet Common Core
Standards in Math, K–7

INTRODUCTION

STUDENT STRUGGLES WITH FRACTIONS

It is well known that students (and adults) struggle with fractions (National Mathematics Advisory Panel, 2008; Noura, 2009; Siegler et al., 2010), so exploring instruction related to fractions becomes particularly important. It is often discouraging when observing student performance on fraction tasks. For example, 67% of 5th-graders and 42% of 9th-graders incorrectly ordered the fractions $\frac{1}{7}$, $\frac{5}{6}$, 1, and $\frac{4}{3}$ (Siegler, Fazio, Bailey, & Zhou, 2013).

One researcher who did a significant amount of study of students' fractional thinking was Kieran (1980). He suggested that underlying any conception of fractions is the concept of part-whole, and he described four different interpretations of fractions: measure, ratio, quotient, and operator (Charalambous & Pitta-Pantazi, 2005). The concept of *operator* is probably closest to the Common Core State Standards for Mathematics (CCSSM) term concept of scaling (or resizing) used to describe multiplication of fractions in Grade 5. The fact that there are these many interpretations of fractions helps explain why representations, comparisons, and operations with fractions are so complex and challenging for students.

Large numbers of students hold many misconceptions about fractions. Some of those common misconceptions are referenced by Mack (1995), McNamara and Shaughnessy (2011), Moss and Case (1999), Stafylidou and Vosniadou (2004), Kamii and Clark (1995), Siegler et al. (2013), and Small (2013). They include:

- conflicts with prior knowledge about whole numbers, such as
  - there is always a specific "next" whole number, but there is no specific next fraction
  - 1 being the smallest number, but then finding out there are smaller numbers
  - multiplication making amounts bigger, but not when multiplying with proper fractions

  ◆ division making amounts smaller, but not when dividing by proper
    fractions
  ◆ 3 being more than 2, but $\frac{1}{3}$ being less than $\frac{1}{2}$; or $\frac{4}{5}$ being more than $\frac{7}{10}$,
    even though 7 and 10 are more than 4 and 5
- too often using faulty perceptual arguments rather than mathematical
  reasoning to compare two fractions
- viewing the numerator and denominator as separate entities (as essentially two numbers), rather than viewing the fraction as a single number
- believing that fractions are always less than 1, perhaps because of the
  early emphasis on fractions as being parts of a whole, which becomes
  problematic once improper fractions are introduced
- errors due to inconsistencies in performing fraction operations (e.g., the
  fact that a common denominator is required for adding and subtracting
  but not for multiplying)
- difficulties with placing fractions on number lines that extend past 1 (e.g.,
  marking the point 2 when asked to place $\frac{1}{2}$ on a number line that extends
  from 0 to 4)
- not recognizing the role that the whole plays in describing a fraction

The suggestions presented in this book are based on the substantial literature
about fraction teaching and learning that has come to recognize that instruction
can make a significant difference in student success with fraction concepts. Although some of the needed improvements are already reflected in the CCSSM, the
delivery of these ideas through appropriate instruction is a crucial element in student understanding. It is believed that the approaches emphasized in this resource
will help support student understanding and minimize misconceptions.

FOCUSING ON MATHEMATICAL PRACTICE

The CCSSM derive from the National Council of Teachers of Mathematics processes (National Council of Teachers of Mathematics, 2000) and the strands of
mathematical proficiency from *Adding It Up* (National Research Council, 2001).
These standards for mathematical practice describe the mathematical environ-
ment in which it is intended that the Common Core State Standards for Mathematics are learned. These standards are meant to influence the instructional stance
that teachers take when presenting mathematical tasks, and are addressed in this
resource both in the underlying ideas presented for each topic and in the types of
good questions suggested.

Listed below are just a few examples of each standard presented in this resource.

1. ***Make sense of problems and persevere in solving them.*** In discussions of operations with fractions in Grades 4, 5, 6, and 7, I focus on analyzing what the different operations mean and how story problems reflect these different operations. An example is in Grade 4, where a section (pp. 52–53) is devoted to the various meanings of subtraction of fractions that might emerge in real-world problems. Students are asked to both solve and create problems that involve computations with fractions. Another example is in the Grade 6 section (p. 100) where students are asked to create a problem solved by dividing $\frac{4}{5}$ by $\frac{2}{3}$.

   The issue of perseverance cannot be dealt with directly in this resource, but it is a value that is important for teachers to encourage and support in the classroom.

2. ***Reason abstractly and quantitatively.*** Reasoning is at the heart of mathematics. As a result, there is a wealth of examples in this resource that focus on helping students reason. A few examples are in the Grade 3 section (pp. 30–31) where students consider why, if two fractions have the same numerator, it is the one with the lesser denominator that is the greater fraction, or in the Grade 2 section (p. 14) where students recognize why the same rectangle can be $\frac{1}{2}$, $\frac{1}{3}$, or $\frac{1}{4}$ of the size of other rectangles.

3. ***Construct viable arguments and critique the reasoning of others.*** Because this resource focuses on making sense of the mathematics of fractions, teachers are frequently encouraged to set up situations where students can make arguments as to why things happen the way they do. One example is in the Grade 2 section (p. 12) where students are asked to create an argument as to why the picture below shows fourths (i.e., the pieces are equal in area).

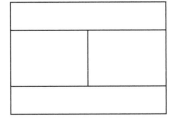

Another example is in the Grade 6 section (p. 97) where students are asked to consider why one can divide by $\frac{a}{b}$ by multiplying by $\frac{b}{a}$. Included in the discussion is the opportunity to critique a provided algebraic argument.

4. ***Model with mathematics.*** There are a number of instances where fractions themselves or operations with fractions model real-world situations. Two examples are discussed in the Grade 5 section. First (pp. 79–80), an exploration of treating fractions as division relates to real-life sharing experiences. Later (pp. 85–86), fraction multiplications are used to solve scaling problems.

5. ***Use appropriate tools strategically.*** Because of the emphasis in this resource on appropriate manipulatives and on students using a variety of strategies, there are many examples that describe the use of appropriate tools strategically. One example is in the Grade 3 section (p. 26) where students use a fraction tower in order to efficiently explore equivalence of fractions, and another is in Grade 5 (pp. 71–73) where a grid model is proposed for addition and subtraction of fractions.

   With a focus on the importance of estimation, there are also a number of examples where teachers are provided guidance regarding how estimation can be used strategically as a tool. Two examples: in the Grade 5 section (p. 75) where estimation is used when adding fractions, and in the Grade 6 section (p. 98) where estimation is used when dividing fractions.

6. ***Attend to precision.*** Precision can often be an issue with fractions when they are being compared, and particularly when students create their own models. An example of this is found in the Grade 3 section (pp. 30–31) where models that represent two different fractions with different denominators at the same time are discussed.

   Precision is also addressed in terms of the notion that one can get increasingly closer and closer to any fraction. This is alluded to in the Grade 3 section (p. 32) where students are asked to create a fraction closer to 1 than a given one that is already close.

7. ***Look for and make use of structure.*** Mathematics is built on structure, and there are many examples where structure is used to draw conclusions. One example discussed in the resource is in the Grade 2 section (p. 14) where students realize that whenever a fraction is modeled, implicitly another fraction is modeled too. Another example is in the Grade 6 section (pp. 97–98) where the relationship between multiplication and division is called upon, and another in the Grade 7 section (pp. 110–111) where the prediction of the sign of the sum of two rational numbers is analyzed.

8. ***Look for and express regularity in repeated reasoning.*** This standard is visible in a number of situations in this resource. One is in the Grade 3 section (p. 24)

where teachers are shown how to help students see that there is no end to the number of equivalent names for a fraction. Another is in the Grade 4 section (p. 59) where teachers help students see how the place value system can be extended to accommodate numbers less than 1.

FOCUSING ON MATHEMATICAL CONTENT

This resource is organized around the specifics of the CCSSM content standards related to instruction about fractions. Most of the specific content standards are listed under Number and Operations—Fractions, but some of them are actually found in other domains (e.g., Number and Operations in Base Ten, Geometry, and Ratio and Proportional Relationships).

SUMMARY

Because of long-documented student struggles with understanding fractions, and especially in light of the new Common Core State Standards for Mathematics, particularly for Mathematical Practice, it is essential for teachers to have an opportunity to deconstruct their own understanding of fractions and, thus, set the stage for students' deeper understanding.

The next sections of this book attempt to make that easier for teachers by digging deeply into the underlying ideas that inform the standards.

GRADE 1

Partitioning Wholes Into Equal Areas

Geometry	CCSSM 1.G
Reason with shapes and their attributes.	

3. Partition circles and rectangles into two and four equal shares, describe the shares using the words *halves*, *fourths*, and *quarters*, and use the phrases *half of*, *fourth of*, and *quarter of.* Describe the whole as two of, or four of the shares. Understand for these examples that decomposing into more equal shares creates smaller shares.

IMPORTANT UNDERLYING IDEAS

> ➤ *Notions of partitioning.* The concept of partitioning (sharing) is fundamental to the notion of fraction as part of a whole. Often students understand partitioning best when presented as a set of objects that is shared, rather than a single object—for example, when 2 children share 6 cookies. Later, students will be able to model a process whereby 2 children share 5 cookies (and need to split one cookie in half). Or students might share 8 cookies among 4 students and later 10 cookies among 4 students (Siegler et al., 2010).

Before long, students might share a single object, for example a circle model representing a pizza, among initially 2 and then 4 students. Notice that the shapes suggested for partitioning in the standard, circles and rectangles, are symmetrical. It is only later that students would be expected to partition nonsymmetrical shapes.

There is research (Petit, Laird, & Marsden, 2010) that suggests that students find it easiest to partition into halves, so partitions of 2, 4, and, later, 8 make sense to start with. At some point students will become comfortable with partitions of, for example, 3 or 5, but not initially. Even later they can use partitions of 3 and 5 to create partitions of 6 and 10.

Early work with partitioning might be set up using plastic fraction pieces where half and quarter pieces are available to place on top of a full circle or rectangle. This allows students to be a bit more precise than they could be with drawings.

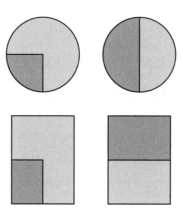

Later students might be provided with images where they draw or fold to estimate equal shares. When partitioning rectangles or circles into 4 equal pieces, it might make sense to initially provide an image of the shape divided into 2 equal parts and ask students to think about how to get from 2 shares to 4 shares. This supports the mathematical practice standards of constructing viable arguments and reasoning abstractly and quantitatively.

An important concept that needs to emerge is that more sharers of the same whole leads to a smaller share for each. This is fundamental not only to an understanding of fractions (e.g., why $\frac{1}{4}$ is less than $\frac{1}{2}$), but also for mastery of other mathematical ideas related to division. For example, more advanced students should realize why $20 \div 5$ must be less than $20 \div 4$, since there are more sharers.

➤ **Using fraction words.** Notice that the standard does not require the use of fraction notation. I would advise starting work with fractions using words and not symbols. This avoids students potentially drawing inappropriate conclusions based on the numbers that they see. For example, we do not want to encourage students to think that $\frac{1}{4} > \frac{1}{2}$ since $4 > 2$. This is less likely to occur if we use the words "*fourth*" (or "*quarter*") and "*half*" than if the symbols are written.

This approach of using words rather than symbols emphasizes that *one half* or *one fourth* is one number. This is an important foundation for ensuring that subsequent work in fractions is well grounded.

> *Recognizing halves and fourths.* Students are apt to recognize halves and fourths of circles even without seeing the wholes, but quick identification is less likely if rectangles are used.

For example, it is obvious that the picture on the left represents half of a circle and the picture on the right a quarter of a circle.

It is much less clear whether the picture below represents half or a quarter of a given rectangle unless the whole rectangle is shown.

However, this should not lead to using circles most of the time. It should instead mean that rectangles are often used in order to help students become aware of the need to know the whole in order to describe a part.

> *Alternate approaches to introducing fractions.* Although the Common Core State Standards for Mathematics suggest introducing fractions through an area model, in other jurisdictions, fractions are introduced first through other measures, such as length or volume (Watanabe, 2006) or through sharing sets (e.g., taking half of a set of candies) (Empson, 1995). For some students, these alternate approaches might make more sense.

Good Questions to Ask

- *Provide two identical circles. Ask students to fold one circle into halves and the other into quarters. Ask students: Which pieces are bigger? Why?*
- *Ask students to describe what the word "half" means.*
- *Ask students if each of the gray sections is one fourth or not. [Some students will be (and should be) disturbed that the right-hand shape is not properly divided, but may still recognize that the gray is still one fourth of the whole since 4 of them would make a whole.]*

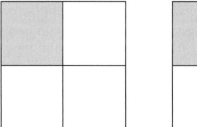 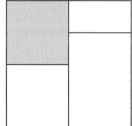

- *Provide geoboards that are 5 pin × 5 pin (16 unit squares) or else a 4 × 4 grid of squares. Ask students to divide the board or grid in half in as many ways as they can.* [Not only can the boards be divided vertically, horizontally and diagonally, but some students may find other ways to split the 16 squares on the board into 2 sections of 8 squares. One is shown below. This is an example of the practice standard: Use appropriate tools strategically.]

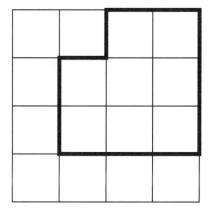

- Ask students: *Draw a picture to show why someone might say that one fourth can be more than one half.* [The idea is to draw two different-sized wholes. The whole for the fourths is much bigger than the whole for the halves.]
- Ask students: *Why is creating 2 equal parts a good first step if you want to create 4 equal parts?*

Summary

By the end of Grade 1, student comfort with partitioning shapes into smaller shapes should support further development in fraction work in Grade 2, but also in work with number in general. Thinking about and performing compositions and decompositions to describe parts of shapes and numbers is a critical element of mathematics learning.

GRADE

Partitioning Wholes Into Equal Areas

Geometry	CCSSM 2.G
Reason with shapes and their attributes.	

3. Partition circles and rectangles into two, three, or four equal shares, describe the shares using the words *halves, thirds, half of, a third of,* etc., and describe the whole as two halves, three thirds, four fourths. Recognize that equal shares of identical wholes need not have the same shape.

IMPORTANT UNDERLYING IDEAS

> ➤ *Recognizing equal shares.* Students should have opportunities to distinguish between shapes that are correctly divided into halves or thirds or fourths and those that are not.

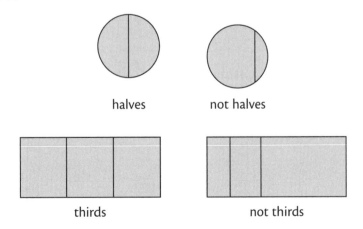

halves   not halves

thirds   not thirds

When creating halves, thirds, or fourths, students at this level are most likely to divide the shape in a simple, consistent way. For example, to show thirds, they might split a rectangle using two vertical lines, as shown above. It would actually be difficult for many students to build thirds out of a circle, although they might well recognize predivided thirds.

> *Checking for identical measures rather than identical shapes.* When rectangles are cut into equal shares, the shares do not have to be identical in shape; they need only be equal in area.

For example, the rectangle below shows 4 equal shares even though the pieces are not identical

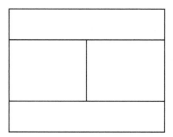

A student might show that the parts are fair shares by taking one of the top or bottom pieces, cutting it in half vertically and stacking the halves to create a piece that looks like a middle piece.

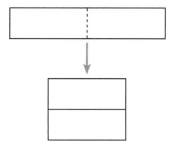

The fourths shown below also have equal areas, but are not identical. Although it is clear that the top and bottom pieces are the same and the left and right pieces are the same, it might be less obvious that all four pieces have the same area.

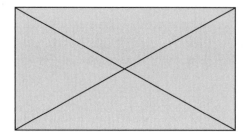

By cutting, for example, the bottom triangle vertically, and then rearranging the two pieces as shown below, a triangle identical to the right one in the picture above can be created, showing that the bottom and right piece must have the same area.

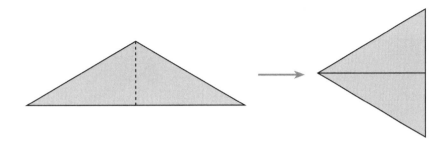

Cutting and rearranging the pieces below shows that each piece is a third of the total area.

Unlike rectangles, when circles are cut into equal shares, the pieces tend to look identical.

➤ *Noticing that the size of the pieces relates to the size of the whole.* By asking students to partition both large and small shapes into halves, thirds, and fourths, students should begin to recognize that the sizes of the shares relate to the size of the whole.

If a large rectangle is halved, then each half is large; if a small rectangle is halved, each half is small.

> ➤ **Noticing that fractions come in pairs.** Students should recognize that whenever one third or one fourth is represented, two thirds or three fourths is also automatically represented as the rest of the whole.

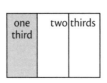 

More generally, whenever any fraction is represented, the rest of the whole is either explicitly or implicitly represented.

> ➤ **Vocabulary issue.** The word *thirds* will probably be new to students in this grade. Care should be taken to clarify what *thirds* means and contrast it with the ordinal number word *third*, which describes where someone might be in a line.

Good Questions to Ask

- *Ask students which of the pictures below show fourths. [The idea is to help them see that the subdivisions need not be identical, but must have the same area. Only the third shape does not show fourths.]*

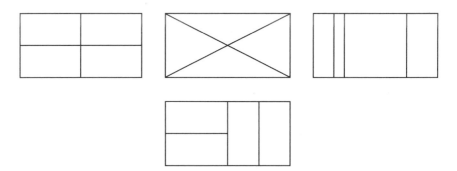

- *Provide only the gray rectangle. Then ask students why it is possible for the exact same rectangle (the gray one) to be half of one rectangle, yet one third or one fourth of another. Students might draw the picture below.*

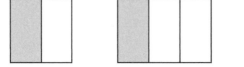 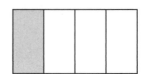

- *Ask students to divide up both a big rectangle and a small one into 4 equal pieces. Ask them whether they think all fourths look the same or not.* [Hopefully, they notice that the fourths in each picture are all the same size, but might be of a different size or have different proportions than the fourths in the other picture.]

Summary

By the end of Grade 2, most students should have become comfortable with the notion that there are many ways to equally divide objects into fractional pieces, the importance of equality of area in that subdivision, and also the role of the whole in describing fractional parts.

This should prepare students for the much more intense and broader examination of fraction meanings that begins in Grade 3.

GRADE 3

Interpreting $\frac{a}{b}$ as Copies of $\frac{1}{b}$

Number and Operations—Fractions	CCSSM 3.NF

Develop understanding of fractions as numbers.

1. Understand a fraction $\frac{1}{b}$ as the quantity formed by 1 part when a whole is partitioned into b equal parts; understand a fraction $\frac{a}{b}$ as the quantity formed by a parts of size $\frac{1}{b}$.

2. Understand a fraction as a number on the number line; represent fractions on a number line diagram.

   a. Represent a fraction $\frac{1}{b}$ on a number line diagram by defining the interval from 0 to 1 as the whole and partitioning it into b equal parts. Recognize that each part has size $\frac{1}{b}$ and that the endpoint of the part based originating at 0 locates the number $\frac{1}{b}$ on the number line.

   b. Represent a fraction $\frac{a}{b}$ on a number line diagram by marking off a lengths $\frac{1}{b}$ from 0. Recognize that the resulting interval has size $\frac{a}{b}$ and that its endpoint locates the number $\frac{a}{b}$ on the number line.

IMPORTANT UNDERLYING IDEAS

> **Fractions as parts of sets.** Although students' introduction to fractions in the Common Core State Standards in 1st grade and 2nd grade focuses on the partitioning of an area, other measures become more significant in 3rd grade. One of these measures is number; in this case, fractions are used to describe parts of sets. For example, $\frac{2}{3}$ means that a set of objects is divided into 3 equal subsets and the number in 2 of those subsets is counted.

The gray counters make up $\frac{2}{3}$ of the set of 12 counters.

A connection could be made between partitioning sets and partitioning shapes by using the partitions of shapes as a model on which to place the counters.

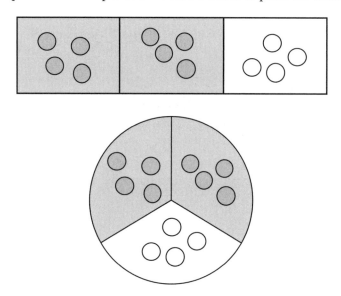

> *Misconceptions students might have about parts of sets.* Many students are uncomfortable suggesting that $\frac{1}{3}$ of the stars on the right are dark, but have no problem believing that $\frac{1}{3}$ of the stars on the left are dark.

In each set of 3, $\frac{1}{3}$ of the number of stars is dark

When using a part-of-set interpretation of fractions, all that matters is the number of items in each subset, not the size of any of the items. When we say, for example, that $\frac{1}{2}$ of a group of people are adults, we do not worry about the exact sizes of those people. This is analogous to the issue of partitioning a whole, where all that matters is the area of the resulting portion, not its exact shape.

Notions of parts of sets apply even if the items are touching. For example, in the design below, one can say that $\frac{2}{3}$ of the shapes in the design are squares, even though one would not say that the two squares make up $\frac{2}{3}$ of the design (in fact, it is $\frac{4}{5}$).

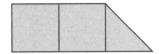

> *Interpreting $\frac{a}{b}$ as a copies of $\frac{1}{b}$ using different fraction models.* It is important that students recognize that $\frac{3}{5}$ means 3 copies of $\frac{1}{5}$. This is true whether the $\frac{1}{5}$ is part of an area, part of a length, part of a set, part of a mass, or part of a volume.

To create an area described by the number $\frac{3}{5}$, students must cut the unit area into 5 pieces with equal area, name each piece one fifth (or $\frac{1}{5}$) and include 3 of them.

To create a length described by the number $\frac{3}{5}$, students must cut the unit length into 5 pieces with equal length, name each piece one fifth (or $\frac{1}{5}$) and use 3 of those pieces. If the length happens to be on a number line, the length cut into 5 equal pieces is the segment between 0 and 1. The number $\frac{3}{5}$, which requires 3 jumps of $\frac{1}{5}$ beginning at 0, is the "address" at the right-hand end point of those adjacent jumps. If a segment were formed attaching 0 to that right-hand end point, that segment would have the length $\frac{3}{5}$ of a unit.

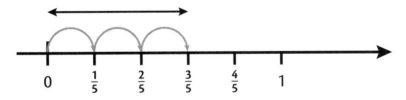

Recognizing number line interpretations of fractions is essential for measuring skills.

To create a set described by the number $\frac{3}{5}$, students must separate the unit set into 5 subsets with the same number of items in each subset, name each subset one fifth (or $\frac{1}{5}$) and include 3 of them. This is true whether 5 items are used or a multiple of 5 items. It is important that students experience both of these situations.

Each heart is $\frac{1}{5}$ of the set. 3 hearts are $\frac{3}{5}$ of the set.

Each column of hearts is $\frac{1}{5}$ of the set.
3 columns of hearts make up $\frac{3}{5}$ of the set.

To create a volume described by the number $\frac{3}{5}$, students must cut the unit solid into 5 pieces with equal volume, name each piece one fifth (or $\frac{1}{5}$) and include 3 pieces.

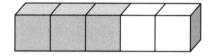

At some point, this understanding of $\frac{3}{5}$ as 3 sets of $\frac{1}{5}$ will help students see why $\frac{15}{5} = 3$ (if there are 15 copies of $\frac{1}{5}$, and each 5 copies of $\frac{1}{5}$ makes a 1, then there are 3 ones). Later on, this understanding will also help students better understand why $\frac{3}{5} \times 2$ is 3 times as much as $\frac{1}{5} \times 2$.

➤ **Misconceptions students might have about representations.** It is important that students realize that unless a fraction is shown as a number on a number line, the "shaded" pieces need not be adjacent. For example, both of the pictures below show $\frac{3}{5}$. Often, students do not realize that the right-hand picture still shows $\frac{3}{5}$, even though the shaded pieces are not adjacent.

➤ **Partitioning shapes more easily.** Many students struggle with breaking up a whole area into equal parts other than halves or fourths.

If students are representing other fractions, or if they are representing two or more fractions with the same denominator, student need to figure out ways to make it easy to more accurately model the fraction(s). For example, to show $\frac{2}{7}$, they might build a shape made of 7 squares or build a 3-D shape made of 7 cubes. However, to show fifths, it might be easier to start with a shape made of 5 or 10 squares or 5 or 10 cubes.

If students must represent two different fractions with different denominators using a single whole, they must choose to either:

1. be less precise, making reasonable estimates

   For example, to show both $\frac{2}{3}$ and $\frac{4}{5}$ on a number line, the student could realize that both fractions are between $\frac{1}{2}$ and 1, but $\frac{2}{3}$ is closer to $\frac{1}{2}$ and $\frac{4}{5}$ is closer to 1. They can "estimate" how long thirds or fifths are.

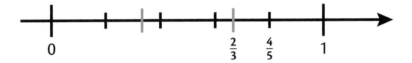

2. or use a whole that is easy to work with for both denominators

   For example, to show both $\frac{2}{3}$ and $\frac{4}{5}$ of a shape, students might build a whole with 15 (3 × 5) pieces. In the situation below, each third is a row and each fifth is a column, so both $\frac{2}{3}$ and $\frac{4}{5}$ are easy to represent.

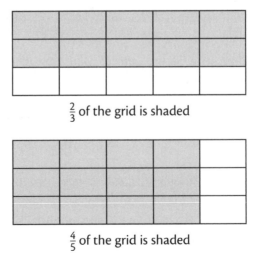

$\frac{2}{3}$ of the grid is shaded

$\frac{4}{5}$ of the grid is shaded

This is an example built on the mathematical practice standard of modeling and selecting tools strategically.

➤ **Fractions as numbers.** Many students think of fractions as two numbers (e.g., $\frac{3}{5}$ as 3 and 5 combined "somehow"). It is important for students to realize that a fraction is a single number. This notion is used when students order fractions, realizing one number is to the right of the other on a number line; when they add them, since numbers are what we add; or when they write fractions as decimals.

Research indicates that students might continue to think of $\frac{1}{2}$ as a portion of a given length or area rather than a number when using a number line, particularly if that number line goes past 1. For example, a student might mark the position of the number $\frac{1}{2}$ at 2 rather than A on the number line shown below, since they are thinking of the full segment (which extends to 4) as the whole, rather than the segment from 0 to 1. This is an example of the need to attend to precision, a mathematical practice standard.

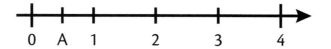

Good Questions to Ask

- *Tell students that Connor has these 3 pieces. Ask what fraction he would be modeling if he put all of the pieces together and how they know.*

- *Ask students why $\frac{2}{3}$ is the name of point A by asking where the 2 comes from and where the 3 comes from.*

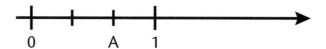

Then ask for other things the picture shows about $\frac{2}{3}$. [They might note that $\frac{2}{3}$ is more than $\frac{1}{2}$, that $\frac{2}{3}$ is closer to $\frac{1}{2}$ than to 1, or just that $\frac{2}{3}$ is less than 1.]
- *Provide students with a rectangle and ask them to cut it into sixths. Then ask them to describe all the different fractions they see in their picture. [Presumably, they can see $\frac{1}{6}, \frac{2}{6}, \frac{3}{6}, \frac{4}{6}, \frac{5}{6}$, and $\frac{6}{6}$; some may even "simplify" to thirds and halves.]*
- *Provide a picture like the one on the next page and ask students to give each part a fractional name in terms of the whole square. [Note that the values from left to right on top are $\frac{1}{8}, \frac{1}{8}, \frac{1}{12}, \frac{1}{12}$, and $\frac{1}{12}$ and on bottom are $\frac{1}{4}, \frac{1}{16}, \frac{1}{16}, \frac{1}{16}$, and $\frac{1}{16}$.]*

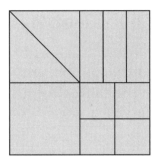

- Provide a number line with labels at 0 and 1 and with markings at each quarter. Ask students to locate the following fractions: $\frac{3}{4}$, $\frac{5}{8}$, $\frac{2}{3}$, and $\frac{1}{10}$.
- Provide a picture like the one below to students. Tell them that each jump size is a fraction of the form $\frac{1}{\square}$. Ask what the number is where the last jump ends. [This will emphasize that if there are 6 jumps, it has to be a fraction with a numerator of 6 or a number equivalent to that fraction (e.g., it could be $\frac{3}{2}$ since $\frac{3}{2} = \frac{6}{4}$, or it could be 3 since $\frac{6}{2} = 3$).]

0   ?

To make the problem even more challenging, change the rules so that the value of ? has to be between $\frac{1}{2}$ and 1.
- Ask students to draw the whole given a part. This can be made more or less challenging depending on the fraction used and the shape used.

This is $\frac{1}{3}$. What does the whole look like? [A student could simply put together 3 of these triangles.]

This is $\frac{2}{5}$. What does the whole look like? [A student could cut the hexagon down a line of symmetry and combine 5 of those half-hexagons.]

This is $\frac{3}{8}$. What does the whole look like? [A student could split the rectangle into 3 equal parts and use 8 of those thirds.]

Equivalent Fractions

Number and Operations—Fractions	CCSSM 3.NF
Develop understanding of fractions as numbers.	

3. Explain equivalence of fractions in special cases, and compare fractions by reasoning about their size.
   a. Understand two fractions as equivalent (equal) if they are the same size, or the same point on a number line.
   b. Recognize and generate simple equivalent fractions, e.g., $\frac{1}{2} = \frac{2}{4}$, $\frac{4}{6} = \frac{2}{3}$. Explain why the fractions are equivalent, e.g., by using a visual fraction model.
   c. Express whole numbers as fractions, and recognize fractions that are equivalent to whole numbers. *Examples:* Express 3 in the form $3 = \frac{3}{1}$; recognize that $\frac{6}{1} = 6$; locate $\frac{4}{4}$ and 1 at the same point of a number line diagram.

IMPORTANT UNDERLYING IDEAS

➤ *Thinking of an equivalent as another name for the same amount.* Students should think of an equivalent fraction as just another name for the same amount. In a way, this is no different than thinking of 20 as 2 tens sometimes but as 1 ten and 10 ones other times, or as 4 groups of 5 at yet other times. We are simply saying that sometimes it is useful to think of a fraction in another form (e.g., $\frac{10}{20}$ as $\frac{1}{2}$), since this helps us imagine it more easily.

Eventually, although not necessarily at this grade level, students need to understand that there are an infinite number of equivalent names for a fraction. This is essentially because one can always subdivide each of the original parts into as many smaller pieces as one might want—an example of the mathematical practice standard of looking for and expressing regularity in repeated reasoning.

Below, the original halves are each subdivided into 2 or 3 or 6 parts, but the halves could have been subdivided into any number of equal parts.

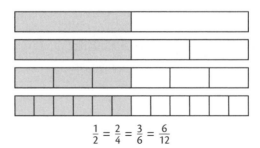

$$\frac{1}{2} = \frac{2}{4} = \frac{3}{6} = \frac{6}{12}$$

> **Beginning with the concrete.** Initially, students should determine fraction equivalence in a concrete way, wherein they overlay one fraction on top of another to see if the two amounts occupy the same space. Pattern blocks are useful materials for representing certain fractions in this way. For example, if the hexagon is the whole, the trapezoid is $\frac{1}{2}$, the parallelogram is $\frac{1}{3}$, and the equilateral triangle is $\frac{1}{6}$.

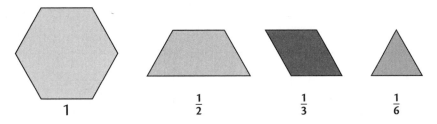

1          $\frac{1}{2}$ $\frac{1}{3}$ $\frac{1}{6}$

Note: It is important to recognize that the names of the pieces would change if a different whole were used. For example, if the trapezoid is the whole, the small triangle represents $\frac{1}{3}$ and not $\frac{1}{6}$.

Students might place parallelogram pattern blocks on top of a hexagon; they see that the parallelogram is $\frac{1}{3}$ of the hexagon and that $\frac{3}{3}$ makes 1.

They then place triangle pattern blocks on top of a hexagon; they see that a triangle is $\frac{1}{6}$ of a hexagon and that $\frac{6}{6}$ makes 1.

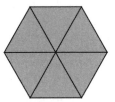

They could cover the parallelogram with 2 triangles and see why $\frac{1}{3} = \frac{2}{6}$.

Students might also use a fraction tower, in which fractions are equivalent if they occupy the same space. Below, we see that $\frac{2}{3} = \frac{4}{6}$.

Students have a choice of simply visualizing or actually cutting out fraction tower pieces and overlaying them to see the equivalence.

Third-graders should be exposed to many similar concrete or pictorial experiences; only much later should the generation of equivalent fractions be presented symbolically, where numerator and denominator are multiplied by the same amount.

Students may make errors if they use part-of-set models to show equivalence. For example, many students look at a part-of-set model for $\frac{1}{2}$ and another for $\frac{2}{4}$ and think that $\frac{2}{4}$ is more.

$\frac{1}{2}$ gray $\frac{2}{4}$ gray

In fact, they may think of $\frac{2}{4}$ as being twice as much as $\frac{1}{2}$. For this reason, part-of-whole models might be a better start for dealing with equivalence.

If using part-of-set models, it might be best to use arrays with the same number of rows (or columns). Notice that in each case below, it is clear that $\frac{1}{2}$ of the rows of stars are gray.

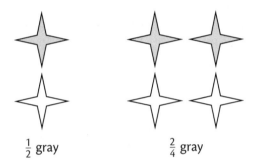

$\frac{1}{2}$ gray $\frac{2}{4}$ gray

➤ **Creating equivalents by partitioning.** Students should recognize that subdividing the pieces of a whole, so that each is subdivided into the same number of pieces, is an effective way to generate equivalent fractions. This is a situation where the mathematical practice standard of looking for and expressing regularity in repeated reasoning comes into play. For example, subdividing thirds into 3 equal pieces results in ninths, but 3 times as many ninths are shaded as thirds were shaded.

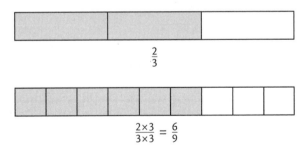

This, in effect, is the same as multiplying numerators and denominators by the same amount; the scale factor is the number of small pieces into which one subdivides each original piece.

➤ **Whole numbers as fractions.** Students should realize that if $\frac{a}{b}$ is a whole number, then either $b = 1$ or else a is a multiple of b. For example, 6 can be written as $\frac{6}{1}$ or $\frac{12}{2}$ or $\frac{18}{3}$, and so on. This concept could be developed by having students think of $\frac{a}{b}$ as a sets of $\frac{1}{b}$. If there are b sets of $\frac{1}{b}$, the value of the fraction ($\frac{b}{b}$) is 1. $n \times b$ sets of $\frac{1}{b}$ (e.g., [4 × 2] sets of $\frac{1}{2}$), can be regrouped into n sets of $\frac{b}{b}$ (e.g., 4 sets of $\frac{2}{2}$), or n sets of 1 (e.g., 4 sets of 1), which is the whole number n (e.g., 4).

Good Questions to Ask

- Ask students to use linking cubes to show why $\frac{2}{3} = \frac{4}{6}$. [They might, for example, use cubes like those shown below, indicating that the light gray and white are $\frac{2}{3}$ of the chain, since there are 3 equal color groups, but these two groups make up $\frac{4}{6}$ of the cubes.]

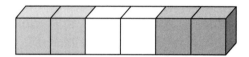

- Ask students how they might predict that $\frac{4}{10}$ cannot possibly be equal to $\frac{10}{12}$. [They could mention the fact that not even half of the first whole is indicated, but almost all of the second whole is, or they could choose to make a model to feel more sure.]
- Ask students whether they believe that the number 1 is a fraction. [Some may rename it as $\frac{2}{2}$ or $\frac{3}{3}$, etc., and call it a fraction if written that way.]
- Ask students how to use a number line to convince someone that $\frac{3}{4} = \frac{6}{8}$. [They might subdivide the segment from 0 to 1 first into fourths and label the appropriate point $\frac{3}{4}$, but then they might subdivide each fourth segment in half and realize that $\frac{3}{4}$ is now $\frac{6}{8}$.]
- Draw a diagram like the one below. Suggest that one student called Point A $\frac{2}{6}$, but another called it $\frac{4}{12}$. Ask who they believe was correct and why.

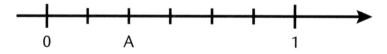

Comparing Fractions

Number and Operations—Fractions	CCSSM 3.NF
Develop understanding of fractions as numbers.	

3. Explain equivalence of fractions in special cases, and compare fractions by reasoning about their size.
   d. Compare two fractions with the same numerator or the same denominator by reasoning about their size. Recognize that comparisons are valid only when the two fractions refer to the same whole. Record the results of comparisons with the symbols >, =, or <, and justify the conclusions (e.g., by using a visual fraction model).

IMPORTANT UNDERLYING IDEAS

> *Visual models for comparison.* Initially, fraction comparison should be visual, either concrete or pictorial. If pattern blocks are used to compare fractions, it is important to establish the same whole before the comparisons are made.

For example, $\frac{2}{3}$ could be made up of two parallelogram pattern blocks if the whole is a hexagon, but only one parallelogram pattern block if the whole is a trapezoid.

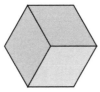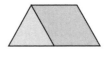

Fractions must be compared using the same whole. In other words, if we ask whether $\frac{3}{4}$ is more or less than $\frac{2}{3}$, we mean $\frac{3}{4}$ compared to $\frac{2}{3}$ of the same whole.

> *Using common denominators.* If two fractions already have the same denominator, it makes sense to compare the numerators. For example, $\frac{5}{6} > \frac{3}{6}$ since 5 > 3. But it should not just be a rule. A student should be thinking: 5 of anything is more than 3 of that same thing; the thing this time is something called one sixth. This builds on work where students recognize that $\frac{a}{b}$ is a copies of $\frac{1}{b}$. Although the visual model can support this reasoning, some students will realize this makes sense strictly from a more abstract number point of view.

Students might also notice that on a number line, $\frac{a}{b} > \frac{c}{b}$ if $a > c$, since more jumps of $\frac{1}{b}$ were taken. For example, $\frac{7}{8}$ is 7 jumps of $\frac{1}{8}$, compared to $\frac{5}{8}$, which is only 5 jumps of $\frac{1}{8}$.

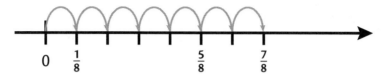

> **Using common numerators.** But if two fractions already have the same numerator, it makes more sense to compare a different way—by appealing to the relative sizes of the individual parts. For example, $\frac{3}{5} > \frac{3}{8}$ since in each instance there are 3 copies of a unit, but one unit ($\frac{1}{8}$) is smaller than the other unit ($\frac{1}{5}$); 3 copies of a larger unit is more than the same number of copies of a smaller unit. This is an example of the mathematical practice of reasoning abstractly and quantitatively.

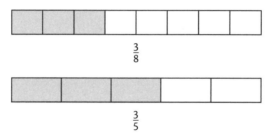

Often students understand best how to compare fractions with common numerators by appealing to their ideas about sharing. Eighths are smaller than fifths since when 8 people share a whole as compared to 5 people sharing the same whole, each person gets less.

Some students might benefit from a grid model to compare fractions with the same numerator but a different denominator. Using a grid makes it easier for them to use the same whole to compare the fractions.

For example, to compare $\frac{3}{5}$ to $\frac{3}{4}$, a student might create two identical 5 × 4 grids to model the two fractions. The two wholes are the same, both made up of 20 equal pieces.

$\frac{3}{5}$ uses up 12 of the 20 pieces:

But $\frac{3}{4}$ uses up 15
of the 20 pieces,
making $\frac{3}{4} > \frac{3}{5}$:

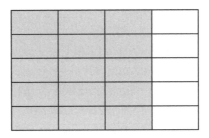

Because there are fewer columns than rows, filling a certain number of columns results in more of the whole than filling the same number of rows.

Many students make errors when comparing fractions with the same numerator but different denominators, assuming that a greater denominator means a greater fraction.

Some of the suggested approaches already shown can be helpful, but some students might benefit by using a fraction tower, which show both of those fractions of the same whole. On the tower, it is easy to see that $\frac{1}{8}$ is smaller than $\frac{1}{6}$, which is why $\frac{5}{8} < \frac{5}{6}$.

1									
$\frac{1}{2}$					$\frac{1}{2}$				
$\frac{1}{3}$			$\frac{1}{3}$			$\frac{1}{3}$			
$\frac{1}{4}$		$\frac{1}{4}$			$\frac{1}{4}$			$\frac{1}{4}$	
$\frac{1}{5}$		$\frac{1}{5}$		$\frac{1}{5}$		$\frac{1}{5}$		$\frac{1}{5}$	
$\frac{1}{6}$		$\frac{1}{6}$		$\frac{1}{6}$		$\frac{1}{6}$		$\frac{1}{6}$	$\frac{1}{6}$
$\frac{1}{8}$	$\frac{1}{8}$	$\frac{1}{8}$	$\frac{1}{8}$		$\frac{1}{8}$	$\frac{1}{8}$		$\frac{1}{8}$	$\frac{1}{8}$
$\frac{1}{9}$	$\frac{1}{9}$	$\frac{1}{9}$	$\frac{1}{9}$	$\frac{1}{9}$	$\frac{1}{9}$	$\frac{1}{9}$		$\frac{1}{9}$	$\frac{1}{9}$
$\frac{1}{10}$	$\frac{1}{10}$	$\frac{1}{10}$	$\frac{1}{10}$	$\frac{1}{10}$	$\frac{1}{10}$	$\frac{1}{10}$	$\frac{1}{10}$	$\frac{1}{10}$	$\frac{1}{10}$

Good Questions to Ask

- *Have students draw a picture to show that $\frac{2}{5} < \frac{2}{3}$. Do not mention that the whole needs to be the same, but observe whether students realize that this is essential.*

- *Ask students to model and name a fraction close to 1. Then ask them to model and name another fraction with either the same numerator or same denominator even closer to 1. Have them tell how they know the second fraction is closer to 1.* [For example, they might choose $\frac{4}{5}$ and $\frac{5}{5}$ or they might choose $\frac{3}{5}$ and $\frac{4}{5}$.]

- *Ask students why, when starting with $\frac{2}{3}$, it is easier to change the denominator than the numerator in order to generate many fractions less than the original $\frac{2}{3}$.* [Ideally, they will realize that they can increase the denominator indefinitely, but can only change the numerator to 0 or 1, assuming they do not consider negative fractions or rational numbers. This is an example of the mathematical practice standard of constructing viable arguments.]

- *Ask students to replace the blanks below in at least three ways to make these statements true. Each time, only one of the right-hand numerator or denominator should change, but not both. Students should explain their thinking for at least one way each time.*

$$\frac{\square}{\square} < \frac{2}{5} \quad \text{[A few possible solutions are } \tfrac{1}{5}, \tfrac{2}{6}, \text{ and } \tfrac{2}{10}.\text{]}$$
$$\frac{\square}{\square} > \frac{2}{6} \quad \text{[A few possible solutions are } \tfrac{3}{6}, \tfrac{4}{6}, \tfrac{2}{5}, \text{ and } \tfrac{2}{4}.\text{]}$$

Partitioning Wholes Into Equal Areas

Geometry	CCSSM 3.G
Reason with shapes and their attributes.	

2. Partition shapes into parts with equal areas. Express the area of each part as a unit fraction of the whole. For example, partition a shape into 4 parts with equal area, and describe the area of each part as $\frac{1}{4}$ of the area of the shape.

IMPORTANT UNDERLYING IDEAS

> *Appropriate wholes to partition.* The concept of using fractions to describe partitions of shape arose in earlier grades, but only with simple rectangular and circular shapes. A broader variety of shapes should be used in Grade 3. These could include shapes like regular hexagons (for sixths) or regular octagons (for eighths), but might involve composite shapes made of simple square pieces, for instance, the shape below to show fifths.

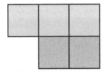

> *Attributes of identical parts of a fraction.* When 2-D or 3-D shapes are cut into equal shares, the shares do not have to be identical in shape; they need only be equal in area or volume.

For example, the white and gray sections on the left-hand shape are both halves of the full shape, since the white and gray areas are equal, even though the two halves are not identical in shape to each other. One can see that the areas are equal by considering the right-hand versions of the shape.

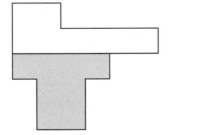 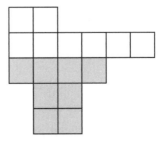

The three shapes below on the left show thirds, since each of the three shapes is made up of three identical squares (shown on the right), but the shapes of the three left-hand pieces are not identical.

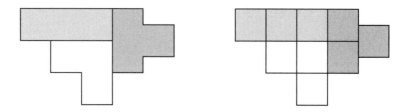

> *Fraction vocabulary.* It is useful to help students see the connection between fraction words (like sixths, fourths, fifths, twelfths) and the cardinal number words (like six, four, five, twelve). It may also be important to distinguish between ordinal numbers and fractions names (e.g., fourth in line means something different than one fourth).

Good Questions to Ask

- *Have students draw or model a variety of shapes to serve as wholes. Ask whether and why (or why not) it takes more fourths to make a whole than it takes thirds to make a whole, or whether it depends on the shape of the whole.*
- *Ask students to draw several different pictures or create several different models to represent tenths. Encourage segments of different lengths as well as various 2-D shapes and/or 3-D shapes. Ask how many tenths it takes to make the whole. Then ask if the number of tenths depends on what the whole is.* [This will indicate whether students realize that the type of whole is irrelevant; it always takes 10 tenths to make a whole.]
- *Ask students to draw pictures to show that sixths can look different, depending on the original whole.* [For example, they might use a hexagon, a rectangle, and a circle and divide each shape into sixths.]

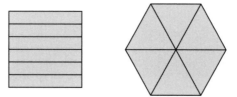

- *Ask students to draw a rectangle and divide it into a lot of equal pieces. They should color in full sections so that almost the whole rectangle is colored and tell*

what fraction is colored. [For example, they might color in $\frac{9}{10}$ or $\frac{7}{8}$ of a rectangle. This focuses students on how, when a fraction is almost 1, the numerator is always close to, but slightly less than, the denominator.]

- *Ask students to consider predivided circles with different numbers of sections. For example, one circle might be divided into four equal sections, but another into eight equal sections, and another into seven equal sections. Then have students color three of the pieces in each and tell the fraction that is colored. Discuss how they figured out the names, what the names had in common (the numerator), and what they did not have in common (the denominator, or how much of the whole is colored in).*

Summary

There is a substantial jump in the amount of fraction work in Grade 2 and Grade 3. By the end of Grade 3, students should have extended their notion of fractions as being part of a whole to fractions as being part of a set, but also of fractions as being numbers on a number line. This understanding of a fraction as a number is critical to making sense of comparisons and operations with fractions.

It is really at this point when many, but not all, students are likely to become more comfortable with symbolic interpretations of fractions.

GRADE 4

Equivalent Fractions

Extend understanding of fraction equivalence and ordering.

1. Explain why a fraction $\frac{a}{b}$ is equivalent to a fraction $(n \times a)/(n \times b)$ by using visual fraction models, with attention to how the number and size of the parts differ even though the two fractions themselves are the same size. Use this principle to recognize and generate equivalent fractions.

IMPORTANT UNDERLYING IDEAS

➢ *Generating equivalent fractions.* In 3rd grade, students began to generate simple equivalent fractions; at the 4th-grade level, the generation of equivalents becomes more general and somewhat more symbolic.

Students should recognize that, by subdividing each of the equal parts of any fraction representation into *n* smaller parts, they have effectively multiplied both the numerator and the denominator by *n*, but they have not changed the value of the fraction. This is an example of the mathematical practice standard of looking for and making use of structure.

For example, the fraction $\frac{2}{5}$ is renamed to $\frac{4}{10}$ when each of the fifths is divided into 2 equal parts. This is because there are now 5×2 parts and 2×2 of them are shaded.

Thinking in reverse, equivalent fractions can be generated by dividing the numerator and the denominator by the same amount. This can be thought of as grouping equal numbers of small parts to create larger parts.

For example, $\frac{2}{8}$ can be thought of as $\frac{1}{4}$ if pairs of the original 8 sections are grouped together. There are half as many sections (so the denominator is half as big) and only half as many are shaded (so the numerator is also half as big).

Some students may look at the multiplicative relationship between the numerator and denominator to decide whether two fractions are equivalent. For example, $\frac{1}{2}$ and $\frac{2}{4}$ are equivalent since, in both cases, the denominator is 2 times the value of the numerator. Thinking in this way, students realize that any fraction equivalent to $\frac{2}{5}$, for example, has a denominator that is $2\frac{1}{2}$ times the value of its numerator, so candidates for equivalent fractions are $\frac{4}{10}$ (since 10 is $2\frac{1}{2} \times 4$) or $\frac{10}{25}$ (since 25 is $2\frac{1}{2} \times 10$).

➤ **Vocabulary attached to equivalence.** Although the term reducing is still used to describe the renaming of a fraction like $\frac{2}{8}$ to $\frac{1}{4}$, I recommend avoiding that term so as to reinforce that the values of $\frac{2}{8}$ and $\frac{1}{4}$ are equal, and that $\frac{1}{4}$ is not less than $\frac{2}{8}$ (because it was reduced). Instead, I suggest renaming to a "simpler form."

Often it is recommended to rename a fraction so that the numerator and denominator have no factors in common (e.g., renaming $\frac{6}{10}$ as $\frac{3}{5}$, since 6 and 10 have a common factor of 2). However, this should depend on the situation. Often we simplify to make a fraction easier to understand, but for many students $\frac{6}{10}$ (which they might think of as more than $\frac{5}{10}$, which is $\frac{1}{2}$) may be easier to comprehend than $\frac{3}{5}$.

Good Questions to Ask

- *Students might be asked to create all the equivalent fractions for $\frac{3}{5}$ that they can where the denominator is less than 20. It would be interesting to see if students use only $\frac{6}{10}$ and $\frac{9}{15}$ or if some students try something like*

$$\frac{7\frac{1}{2}}{12\frac{1}{2}},$$

which is technically a valid fraction.

- *Tell students that Connor ate $\frac{8}{12}$ of a pizza and that Jennifer ate the same amount of the same size pizza, but that she used a different fraction to describe how much she ate. Ask what fraction they think Jennifer probably used. Note that it is possible to either simplify (to, for example, $\frac{2}{3}$ or $\frac{4}{6}$) or to go up (to $\frac{16}{24}$, $\frac{24}{36}$, etc.).*
- *Ask students why equivalent fractions for $\frac{3}{7}$ have either an even numerator and an even denominator or an odd numerator and an odd denominator.* [This assumes, of course, whole number numerators and denominators. This is an example of the mathematical practice standard of constructing viable arguments.]
- *Ask students whether they believe that $\frac{\square}{8}$ can ever be equivalent to $\frac{\square}{20}$.* [This is particularly interesting since 20 is not a multiple of 8, but both 8 and 20 are multiples of 4, so the fractions could have been $\frac{2}{8}$ and $\frac{5}{20}$, for example.]
- *Ask students to determine an equivalent fraction for $\frac{3}{5}$ where the numerator and denominator are 12 apart (the answer is $\frac{18}{30}$). Then ask whether there is an equivalent fraction to $\frac{3}{5}$ where the numerator and denominator are 15 apart.* [There is not. Hopefully, students will observe that numerators and denominators of equivalents to $\frac{3}{5}$ are always a multiple of 2 apart since 3 and 5 are 2 apart. This is an example of the mathematical practice standard of looking for and making use of structure.]

Comparing Fractions

Number and Operations—Fractions	CCSSM 4.NF
Extend understanding of fraction equivalence and ordering.	

2 . Compare two fractions with different numerators and different denominators, e.g., by creating common denominators or numerators, or by comparing to a benchmark fraction such as $\frac{1}{2}$. Recognize that comparisons are valid only when the two fractions refer to the same whole. Record the results of comparisons with symbols >, =, or <, and justify the conclusions, e.g., by using a visual fraction model.

IMPORTANT UNDERLYING IDEAS

> *Choosing equivalent fractions to compare two fractions.* Students can use what they know about equivalent fractions to make it easier to compare two fractions that have both different numerators and different denominators. Whether students choose to create common denominators or common numerators might depend on the situation.

For example, to compare $\frac{4}{5}$ and $\frac{7}{10}$, it might make sense to rename $\frac{4}{5}$ as $\frac{8}{10}$ and then compare $\frac{8}{10}$ to $\frac{7}{10}$.

However, to compare $\frac{4}{5}$ and $\frac{2}{3}$, it might be more efficient to rename $\frac{2}{3}$ as $\frac{4}{6}$. Students know, from previous work, that $\frac{4}{6} < \frac{4}{5}$ since sixths are smaller than fifths, so four sixths is less than four fifths.

It is always possible to either create two equivalent fractions with common denominators (e.g., $\frac{12}{15}$ and $\frac{10}{15}$ for $\frac{4}{5}$ and $\frac{2}{3}$) or two equivalent fractions with common numerators (e.g., $\frac{4}{5}$ and $\frac{4}{6}$ for $\frac{4}{5}$ and $\frac{2}{3}$, as noted above), so the choice should always be with the student. However, they should realize that when one approach requires renaming only one fraction and the other approach requires renaming two fractions, they might find it easier to choose the strategy requiring less renaming.

> *Using a fraction tower.* Although many adults believe that fractions can or should only be compared by using a common denominator, many educators realize that there are a variety of strategies students should use to compare fractions.

A very useful model for fraction comparison is a fraction tower. This allows students to compare many fractions. It is easy to see, for example, why $\frac{3}{4} < \frac{5}{6}$ since $\frac{5}{6}$ extends farther from the left on the tower. This could be shown by using a vertical line to mark the end of each fraction amount. Any two fractions with denominators that appear on the tower can easily be compared using this tool.

> *Comparing fractions by relating numerators to denominators.* Students might compare fractions using the relationship between numerator and denominator. For example, they should realize that any fraction with a greater numerator than denominator (e.g., $\frac{6}{5}$) is greater than a fraction with a greater denominator than numerator (e.g., $\frac{5}{6}$), since the first fraction is greater than a whole and the second is less than a whole.

Students might compare fractions like $\frac{1}{10}$ to $\frac{6}{7}$ by simply realizing that 1 part out of 10 is hardly any of the 10 parts making up the whole, whereas 6 parts out of 7 is almost all of the 7 parts making up the whole.

Therefore, the first fraction is much smaller (closer to 0) than the second (closer to 1). Although initially this should be supported visually, this sort of logical reasoning might be used by a number of students without the visual support.

> ***Using benchmarks to compare fractions.*** Students might compare fractions like $\frac{3}{7}$ and $\frac{5}{8}$ by realizing that $\frac{3}{7}$ must be less than $\frac{1}{2}$ (since one half of 7 is more than 3) whereas $\frac{5}{8}$ must be greater than $\frac{1}{2}$ (since $\frac{4}{8}$ is already one half and $\frac{5}{8}$ is more than $\frac{4}{8}$). In this case, a "benchmark" of $\frac{1}{2}$ is used.

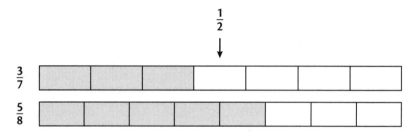

> ***Assuming the same whole when comparing.*** It is critical for students to understand that when we say that one fraction is greater than another, we assume the wholes are the same. Students easily realize that $\frac{1}{4}$ of a very large amount (e.g., of a cake that would feed 50 people) is a lot more than $\frac{1}{2}$ of a very small amount (e.g., of a cookie that would feed 2 people). When we write $\frac{1}{2} > \frac{1}{4}$, the whole we are implying (for both fractions) is the number 1.

Certain fraction models involving comparison confuse students more than other models. For example, if students use blocks to create a model for $\frac{3}{5}$ and a model for $\frac{3}{6}$, they might assume that $\frac{3}{5} = \frac{3}{6}$ since both are made up of 3 blocks. What cannot be overlooked is that the wholes are different.

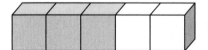

> ***Potential difficulties with improper fractions.*** At this grade level, students are likely to begin to deal with improper fractions—fractions greater than 1. Of course,

they need to be introduced to the vocabulary: improper fraction. Work with improper fractions is often a challenge for students for several reasons.

First, they have been led to believe that fractions are parts of wholes, so they often find it difficult to accept the notion that a fraction can be more than 1.

The other challenge is in the representations. For example, the picture below that is intended to represent $\frac{6}{5}$ is often considered to be $\frac{6}{10}$ by students.

That is because there is insufficient emphasis on the fact that the whole is one of the rectangles, not both. Because the whole is intended to be only one rectangle, each of the gray sections is $\frac{1}{5}$, not $\frac{1}{10}$. To avoid this type of error, teachers might encourage students to mark the whole in some way each time. For example, for the picture above, the student might circle one whole or label it.

one whole

Another approach to clarify the meaning of improper fractions is to focus on a fraction line model, where, for instance, $\frac{6}{5}$ means 6 jumps of $\frac{1}{5}$ from 0. This usually leads to fewer misinterpretations than area models do when dealing with improper fractions.

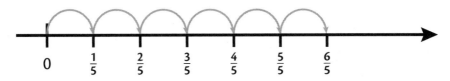

> **Potential comparison problems with self-constructed models.** Care must be taken when students are asked to compare fractions based on their own visual models (ones that are not preconstructed). If the fractions are close in size and student models are rough sketches, the students might well draw incorrect conclusions. For example, a student might judge that $\frac{3}{8} < \frac{1}{3}$ using the model below on the left, but we know it should be more than $\frac{1}{3}$ (as shown in the picture on the right). To avoid this, it might be safer to use preconstructed models for comparisons, only allowing students to draw their own models when representing fractions, but not when comparing them, or only when the fractions being compared are quite

different in size. This ties in to the mathematical practice standard of attending to precision.

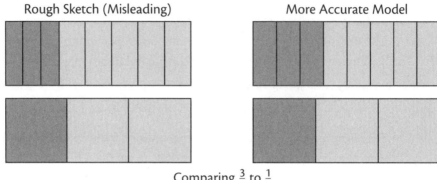

Comparing $\frac{3}{8}$ to $\frac{1}{3}$

> *Misconceptions about comparison based on separately examining numerators and denominators.* Some students have the misconception that $\frac{a}{b} > \frac{c}{d}$ if $a > c$ and $b > d$; in other words, they think that a fraction with both a greater numerator and a greater denominator than another fraction has to be greater than that second fraction.

Although this is sometimes true (e.g., 9 > 4 and 10 > 5 and $\frac{9}{10} > \frac{4}{5}$), it is not always true (e.g., 3 > 1 and 8 > 2, but $\frac{3}{8}$ is not greater than $\frac{1}{2}$). To assure that this misconception does not become entrenched, students could be challenged to find situations where greater numerators and denominators do lead to greater fractions and others where they do not. This is less likely to be a problem, though, if students have a good understanding of fractions, realizing that a fraction represents one number, not two. Notice that this is an example of the mathematical practice standard of creating viable arguments.

Students also often look at how far apart numerators and denominators are to decide which is greater. They believe that if the numerator and denominator are closer in quantity, then the fraction is greater. This conclusion makes sense based on exploration of a fairly limited number of fractions. Again, this is only sometimes true. For example, even though $\frac{9}{10} > \frac{3}{8}$ (the first numerator and denominator are 1 apart and the second numerator and denominator 5 apart), it is not true that $\frac{9}{10} > \frac{95}{100}$ (where, again, the first numerator and denominator are 1 apart and the second numerator and denominator are 5 apart).

> *Density of fractions.* Although not in a formal way, it is important that students understand that between any two fractions there is another one. This is referred to as density. Students should be able to see, for example, that between $\frac{2}{3}$ and $\frac{3}{4}$ there

is space on the number line. To determine the names of fractions that fit in that space, they might get equivalent fractions with either common denominators ($\frac{16}{24}$ and $\frac{18}{24}$) or common numerators ($\frac{12}{18}$ and $\frac{12}{16}$) in order to help them, in this case to figure out that two solutions are $\frac{17}{24}$ or $\frac{12}{17}$. It turns out that another strategy is to add the numerators and the denominators (e.g., $\frac{5}{7}$ is also between $\frac{2}{3}$ and $\frac{3}{4}$).

Good Questions to Ask

- *Ask students how they know that $\frac{2}{10} < \frac{3}{5}$.* [Note that some students might use common denominators but others might use comparisons to one half.]
- *Ask students to choose any digit from 0–6 for each blank and then order the fractions from least to greatest.* [A rich discussion can ensue since it is likely that many choices of fractions will be made.]

$$\frac{\square}{3} \qquad \frac{2}{3} \qquad \frac{2}{\square} \qquad \frac{\square}{5} \qquad \frac{\square}{8}$$

- *Tell students that one fraction is slightly more than $\frac{1}{2}$ and another one slightly less. Ask what the two fractions might be.*
- *Ask students why $\frac{3}{10}$ is not greater than $\frac{1}{2}$ even though 3 > 1 and 10 > 2.*
- *Ask students to select three fractions that they would find easy to compare to $\frac{2}{3}$ and to explain why the comparisons are easy for them.* [This will give good insight into student understanding.]
- *Ask students to name three fractions between $\frac{3}{5}$ and $\frac{9}{10}$. (Examples are $\frac{3}{4}$, $\frac{8}{10}$, $\frac{4}{5}$, $\frac{9}{13}$, etc.) Then ask if they think that there are any pairs of fractions where there are no fractions between them.* [The answer is no, but some students might think there is nothing between $\frac{3}{5}$ and $\frac{4}{5}$. In fact, there is

$$\frac{3\frac{1}{2}}{5},$$

which is another name for $\frac{7}{10}$, as well as many other fractions.]

Relating Fractions and Mixed Numbers

Number and Operations—Fractions	CCSSM 4.NF

Build fractions from unit fractions by applying and extending previous understandings of operations on whole numbers.

3. Understand a fraction $\frac{a}{b}$ with $a > 1$ as a sum of fractions $\frac{1}{b}$.

   b. Decompose a fraction into a sum of fractions with the same denominator in more than one way, recording each decomposition by an equation. Justify decompositions, e.g., by using a visual fraction model. *Examples:* $\frac{3}{8} = \frac{1}{8} + \frac{1}{8} + \frac{1}{8}$; $\frac{3}{8} = \frac{1}{8} + \frac{2}{8}$; $2\frac{1}{8} = 1 + 1 + \frac{1}{8} = \frac{8}{8} + \frac{8}{8} + \frac{1}{8}$.

IMPORTANT UNDERLYING IDEAS

> ➤ ***Thinking of a mixed number as a sum.*** Students need to be introduced to the notation of mixed numbers. There is no obvious reason to know that $2\frac{1}{3} = 2 + \frac{1}{3}$ without being told so.

> ➤ ***Renaming mixed numbers as improper fractions.*** Once students realize that $2\frac{1}{3} = 2 + \frac{1}{3}$, they should realize why $2\frac{1}{3}$ can be rewritten as $\frac{3}{3} + \frac{3}{3} + \frac{1}{3} = \frac{7}{3}$. Although it might be tempting to quickly introduce the rule that a mixed number can be renamed as an improper fraction by multiplying the whole number by the denominator and adding the result to the numerator in order to calculate the numerator of the improper fraction, it is best to allow students to think through the equivalence slowly and in stages, so that eventually it becomes intuitive.

>   For example, to rename $3\frac{5}{8}$ as an improper fraction, students should think: There are $\frac{8}{8}$ in the first 1, $\frac{8}{8}$ in the second 1, and $\frac{8}{8}$ in the third 1, as well as 5 more eighths. This leads to $\frac{8}{8} + \frac{8}{8} + \frac{8}{8} + \frac{5}{8}$, or $\frac{(3 \times 8) + 5}{8}$, or $\frac{29}{8}$. Notice that the numerator of the improper fraction included 3×8 since there were 3 groups of 8 eighths.

Similarly, to rename $4\frac{2}{5}$, the numerator of the improper fraction is $(4 \times 5) + 2$, since there are 4 groups of 5 fifths making up the 4 wholes, plus 2 more fifths, for a solution of $\frac{22}{5}$. This type of analysis supports the mathematical practice standard of reasoning abstractly and quantitatively.

> ***Renaming improper fractions as mixed numbers.*** Some students will notice that the reverse of the above is also possible—one can divide the numerator of an improper fraction by the denominator in order to determine the mixed number name. For example, $\frac{13}{3} = 4\frac{1}{3}$. The reason is that 3 thirds are used to make each 1 whole. Since there are 4 sets of 3 thirds in $\frac{12}{3}$, we are effectively dividing 13 by 3 to determine the number of wholes. There is, of course, still $\frac{1}{3}$ left over.

A number line model might be helpful for some students to see the 12 jumps being divided into groups of 3 jumps, explaining why the numerator is divided by 3.

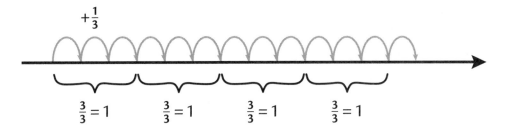

A circle model might be useful to help students see why, for example, $\frac{10}{3} = 3\frac{1}{3}$. If a student uses a part of a set model for a fraction, he or she could see that 10 counters can be distributed equally among the 3 thirds, so that each third contains 3 full counters and $\frac{1}{3}$ of the last counter. It is because the circle model is used that students can see the extra $\frac{1}{3}$ in each of the third sections.

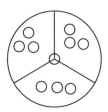

Good Questions to Ask

- Ask students to draw a picture to show why $2\frac{2}{5} = \frac{12}{5}$.
- Provide a number line with labels at 0, 1, 2, 3, and 4 and with markings at each half. Ask students to locate the following fractions: $\frac{3}{4}$, $2\frac{1}{2}$, $1\frac{1}{3}$, and $\frac{8}{9}$.

- *Ask students what these mixed numbers have in common: $3\frac{2}{3}$, $2\frac{3}{4}$, $2\frac{1}{5}$.* [Some students might notice that each can be represented with 11 unit jumps on a number line or 11 fractional pieces or that the improper fraction representation has a numerator of 11. Others might provide simpler answers (e.g., all are more than 1, all are less than 5, etc.).]

- *Ask students to choose different pairs of values for the blanks and to then write the mixed number $\square\frac{\square}{8}$ as an improper fraction.*

- *Tell students that a certain improper fraction can be written as a mixed number in the form $\square\frac{1}{\square}$. Ask what the improper fraction might be. Encourage at least several possibilities.*

Adding and Subtracting Fractions with the Same Denominator

Number and Operations—Fractions	CCSSM 4.NF
Build fractions from unit fractions by applying and extending previous understandings of operations on whole numbers.	

3. Understand a fraction $\frac{a}{b}$ with $a > 1$ as a sum of fractions $\frac{1}{b}$.

   a. Understand addition and subtraction of fractions as joining and separating parts referring to the same whole.

   c. Add and subtract mixed numbers with like denominators, e.g., by replacing each mixed number with an equivalent fraction, and/or by using properties of operations and the relationship between addition and subtraction.

   d. Solve word problems involving addition and subtraction of fractions referring to the same whole and having like denominators, e.g., by using visual fraction models and equations to represent the problem.

IMPORTANT UNDERLYING IDEAS

> ➤ *Looking at a fraction model as implicitly a sum or difference.* Students should recognize that any representation of a fraction can be viewed as a sum or difference of two other fractions.

For example, the representation of $\frac{5}{6}$ below shows that $\frac{5}{6} = \frac{1}{6} + \frac{1}{6} + \frac{1}{6} + \frac{1}{6} + \frac{1}{6}$.

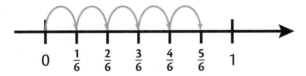

Changing the coloring a bit helps to show why $\frac{5}{6}$ is also $\frac{2}{6} + \frac{3}{6}$.

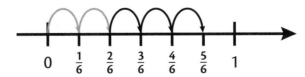

Alternately, $\frac{5}{6}$ could be thought of as $1 - \frac{1}{6}$ or $\frac{8}{6} - \frac{3}{6}$.

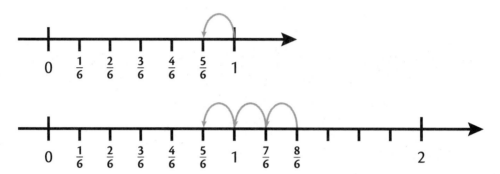

Therefore, one way to introduce the addition and subtraction of fractions is to begin with representations of fractions, rather than with problems involving combining or separating.

> **Thinking of units when adding fractions.** At this level, students are adding and subtracting fractions with like denominators. This focuses students on the meaning of the operations and processes rather than simply on procedures.

When they add fractions (proper or improper) with the same denominator, (e.g., b), students are thinking of the fractions as whole number copies of the unit $\frac{1}{b}$. When adding some copies of $\frac{1}{b}$ to other copies of $\frac{1}{b}$, the total is the total number of copies of $\frac{1}{b}$; it is for this reason that the numerators are added, but the denominators are not.

For example, $\frac{3}{5} + \frac{9}{5}$ means 3 fifths + 9 fifths. Since there are a total of 12 fifths, the sum is $\frac{12}{5}$.

To see that this is actually $2\frac{2}{5}$, it might help students to move one of the light grey pieces from the $\frac{3}{5}$ to complete the second whole used to show $\frac{9}{5}$.

Although technically, adding fractions with like denominators can be thought of as an application of the distributive principle (i.e., that $a(b + c) = ab + ac$, where

$a = \frac{1}{5}$, $b = 3$, and $c = 9$), most students better understand the concept using the following line of thinking: Just like 3 dogs + 9 dogs is 12 dogs, or 3 candies + 9 candies is 12 candies, or 3 children + 9 children is 12 children, 3 fifths + 9 fifths is 12 fifths. This is an example of the mathematical practice of looking for and making use of structure.

> **Thinking of units when subtracting fractions.** Subtraction of proper or improper fractions is built on the same sort of thinking. For example, $\frac{8}{3} - \frac{5}{3}$ might describe a situation where there were 8 copies of $\frac{1}{3}$ and 5 copies were removed. This leaves 3 copies of $\frac{1}{3}$, which is $\frac{3}{3}$, or 1.

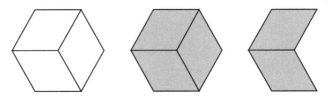

Again, because the unit is constant, it is the numerators that are subtracted and the result is the number of copies of $\frac{1}{3}$; the denominator remains 3.

An alternate way to approach $\frac{8}{3} - \frac{5}{3}$ is to consider what to add to the lesser amount ($\frac{5}{3}$) to get to the greater one ($\frac{8}{3}$). Students could show $\frac{5}{3}$ on a number line and then see what needs to be added to it to get to $\frac{8}{3}$.

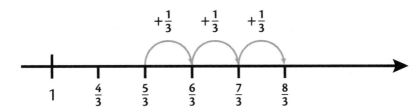

Or they could think: 5 thirds + ? thirds = 8 thirds and realize they need to figure out what to add to 5 to get 8.

> **Common misconceptions about adding.** Because of students' greater comfort with whole numbers than fractions, when they see a calculation such as $\frac{2}{3} + \frac{1}{3}$, it is natural for them to add numerators and add denominators to get $\frac{3}{6}$. Hopefully, if students have been encouraged to estimate, they would realize that it is impossible to start with more than $\frac{1}{2}$ (which $\frac{2}{3}$ is), add a positive amount, and end up with $\frac{3}{6}$, which is $\frac{1}{2}$.

It actually turns out that adding the numerators and denominators of two fractions always results in a fraction between the two original ones. For example, consider the three fractions $\frac{2}{5}$, $\frac{3}{4}$, and $\frac{2+3}{5+4} = \frac{5}{9}$. $\frac{5}{9}$ is between $\frac{2}{3}$ and $\frac{3}{4}$. This should cue students to the error, since the sum should be greater than both of the fractions that are being added when both are positive.

> **Adding or subtracting mixed numbers.** Students often add mixed numbers by renaming each number as an improper fraction and then applying the ideas described above. That is certainly one option. But the downside is that students can better estimate the result if the values are left as mixed numbers.

For example, it is clear that $3\frac{1}{4} + 2\frac{2}{4}$ is between 5 and 6. It is less immediately obvious that $\frac{13}{4} + \frac{10}{4}$ is about 6.

If the student leaves the values as mixed numbers, she or he learns to add the whole number parts together and the fraction parts together, and then to add those results together. For example, $5\frac{1}{3} + 3\frac{2}{3} = 8 + \frac{3}{3}$. Since $\frac{3}{3} = 1$, the student can rename the sum as 9.

To subtract mixed numbers, students could separately subtract the whole number parts and the fraction parts, as long as the greater number's fractional part is greater than the lesser one's. For example, $4\frac{3}{5} - 1\frac{1}{5} = 3\frac{2}{5}$ since $4 - 1 = 3$ and $\frac{3}{5} - \frac{1}{5} = \frac{2}{5}$. If, however, the lesser value has a greater fraction part, a student has to use a variation of this technique.

The student might add up. For example, for $6\frac{2}{8} - 4\frac{5}{8}$, the student might figure out what to add to $4\frac{5}{8}$ to get to $6\frac{2}{8}$. Using a number line can be helpful. The student marks in the lesser number and uses simple whole number benchmarks between the lesser number and the greater number to add in stages. In this case, in total, the student adds $\frac{3}{8} + 1 + \frac{2}{8}$, which is the same as $1 + \frac{3}{8} + \frac{2}{8} = 1\frac{5}{8}$.

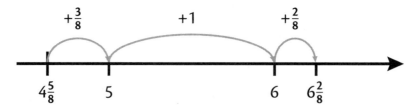

Alternately, the student might think of $6\frac{2}{8}$ as $5 + \frac{10}{8}$ and then subtract $4\frac{5}{8}$. The result would be $(5 - 4)$ added to $\frac{10}{8} - \frac{5}{8}$, or $1\frac{5}{8}$. For many students, this is more challenging than using the adding-up model.

> **Meanings of subtraction when working with fractions.** Word problems involving combining fractions or mixed numbers with like denominators can be approached using the strategies described above. Subtraction word problems can involve any of these meanings of subtraction:

- take-away
- missing addend (What do I have to add?)
- comparison (How much more is ___ than ___?)

Depending on the meaning, it is often helpful for students to model the computation in a way that is consistent with the meaning of subtraction in the problem being solved.

For example, if the problem asked how many cups of sugar are left if there are $2\frac{2}{3}$ cups to start with and the baker uses $1\frac{2}{3}$ cups, students might separately subtract the whole numbers and the fractions, thinking take-away.

If the problem asked how many more cups of sugar are needed if there are $1\frac{2}{3}$ cups available but $2\frac{1}{3}$ cups are needed, adding up might make sense.

If the problem asked how many more cups of flour than sugar are used if the baker uses $3\frac{1}{4}$ cups of flour and $1\frac{3}{4}$ cups of sugar, the student might add up or might model both fractions to see how much more one is than the other.

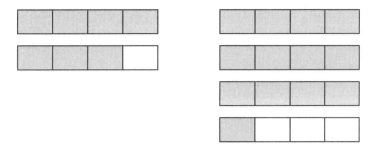

The student can see that, in the model on the right, there is 1 more whole and 2 more fourths than in the model on the left.

Good Questions to Ask

- *Ask students to think of four pairs of fractions, so that each pair adds up to $\frac{12}{5}$. Then ask for four pairs of fractions that sum to $\frac{12}{7}$.* [Observe whether, if they used fractions of the form $\frac{\square}{5}$ in the first problem, they realize that they can use the same numerators and simply replace the 5s with 7s to solve the second problem.]
- *Ask students to explain why there are more pairs of fractions with denominators of 5 that they could subtract to end up with $\frac{4}{5}$ than there are pairs with denominators of 5 that could be added to end up with $\frac{4}{5}$.* [Ideally, assuming they use positive fractions, they will realize that the only pairs that add to $\frac{4}{5}$ are $\frac{0}{5} + \frac{4}{5}$, $\frac{1}{5} + \frac{3}{5}$, and $\frac{2}{5} + \frac{2}{5}$, but that they could use $\frac{5}{5} - \frac{1}{5}$, $\frac{6}{5} - \frac{2}{5}$, $\frac{7}{5} - \frac{3}{5}$, etc. to subtract. This task supports the mathematical practice standard of looking for and making use of structure.]

- Ask students to describe four pairs of mixed numbers that add to a sum of just a little more than 5. (For example, $3\frac{1}{5} + 2$ or $1\frac{3}{4} + 3\frac{2}{4}$.) Then ask for four pairs that sum to just a little less than 5. (For example, $3\frac{1}{5} + 1\frac{3}{5}$ or $2\frac{4}{5} + 2$.)
- Ask students to draw two different pictures that would help someone figure out what $\frac{12}{5} - \frac{4}{5}$ is. [Perhaps one might show take-away and one might show adding up. Or perhaps different models would be used.]
- Ask students to write a story problem to match the computation $3\frac{3}{4} - 2\frac{1}{4}$.

Multiplying Fractions by Whole Numbers

Number and Operations—Fractions	CCSSM 4.NF

Build fractions from unit fractions by applying and extending previous understandings of operations on whole numbers.

4. Apply and extend previous understandings of multiplication to multiply a fraction by a whole number.

   a. Understand a fraction $\frac{a}{b}$ as a multiple of $\frac{1}{b}$. For example, use a visual fraction model to represent $\frac{5}{4}$ as the product $5 \times \frac{1}{4}$, recording the conclusion by the equation $\frac{5}{4} = 5 \times \frac{1}{4}$.

   b. Understand a multiple of $\frac{a}{b}$ as a multiple of $\frac{1}{b}$, and use this understanding to multiply a fraction by a whole number. For example, use a visual fraction model to express $3 \times \frac{2}{5}$ as $6 \times \frac{1}{5}$, recognizing this product as $\frac{6}{5}$. (In general, $n \times \frac{a}{b} = \frac{n \times a}{b}$.)

   c. Solve word problems involving multiplication of a fraction by a whole number, e.g., by using visual fraction models and equations to represent the problem. For example, if each person at a party will eat $\frac{3}{8}$ of a pound of roast beef, and there will be 5 people at the party, how many pounds of roast beef will be needed? Between what two whole numbers does your answer lie?

IMPORTANT UNDERLYING IDEAS

> *Interpreting the meaning of multiplication.* When multiplying whole numbers by fractions, students can call on their understanding of what multiplication means with whole numbers. For instance, they often think of 4×3 as 4 groups of 3. However, they might also think of 4×3 as the result of adding 4 threes or perhaps the amount that is 4 times as much as 3. With that notion, $3 \times \frac{4}{5}$ would mean any of:

- adding $\frac{4}{5}$ 3 times ($\frac{4}{5} + \frac{4}{5} + \frac{4}{5}$)
- 4 fifths + 4 fifths + 4 fifths = 12 fifths, or $\frac{12}{5}$
- the result of three jumps of $\frac{4}{5}$ on a number line, beginning at 0

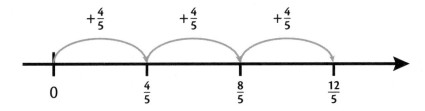

- the number of fifths of a 2-D or 3-D shape if 3 groups of 4 fifths are shaded or colored or filled

Each model will help students see why the result is $\frac{4\times3}{5}$. Using models in this way will help support the mathematical practice standard of looking for and expressing regularity in repeating reasoning.

➤ *Thinking of a single fraction as a product.* Based on earlier work, students should recognize that a fraction like $\frac{4}{5}$ means 4 groups of $\frac{1}{5}$. They might now write this as $\frac{4}{5} = 4 \times \frac{1}{5}$. This directly relates to their understanding of the link between repeated addition and multiplication.

➤ *The difference between* $\mathbf{a} \times \frac{\mathbf{b}}{\mathbf{c}}$ *and* $\frac{\mathbf{b}}{\mathbf{c}} \times \mathbf{a}$. Although we want students to realize that multiplication is commutative and that the order does not matter, the meanings of $5 \times \frac{2}{3}$ and $\frac{2}{3} \times 5$ are somewhat different. The latter is dealt with in Grade 5.

Good Questions to Ask

- *Some students think that* $4 \times \frac{2}{9} = \frac{4\times2}{4\times9}$. *Ask students to decide how they would explain why this is not correct.* [One possibility is to realize that $\frac{8}{36}$ actually is $\frac{2}{9}$ and not 4 groups of $\frac{2}{9}$. Another is simply to realize that $\frac{8}{36}$ just doesn't look like enough, even without noticing it is actually equivalent to $\frac{2}{9}$.]
- *Suggest to students that a certain fraction was multiplied by a certain whole number and that the result was* $\frac{24}{25}$. *Ask what the fraction and the whole number might have been.* [Possibilities include $2 \times \frac{12}{25}$, $4 \times \frac{6}{25}$, $12 \times \frac{2}{25}$, etc.]
- *Point out how* $\frac{4}{5}$ *can be written as* $2 \times \frac{2}{5}$. *Ask students to explain why any fraction can be written as the product of a whole number and a fraction.* [Note that even $\frac{1}{5}$ can be written as either $2 \times \frac{1}{10}$ or simply as $1 \times \frac{1}{5}$.]

Interpreting Decimals

Number and Operations—Fractions	**CCSSM 4.NF**

Understand decimal notation for fractions, and compare decimal fractions.

5. Express a fraction with denominator 10 as an equivalent fraction with denominator 100, and use this technique to add two fractions with respective denominators of 10 and 100. For example, express $\frac{3}{10}$ as $\frac{30}{100}$, and add $\frac{3}{10}$ to $\frac{4}{100}$ to get $\frac{34}{100}$.

6. Use decimal notation for fractions with denominators of 10 or 100. For example, rewrite 0.62 as $\frac{62}{100}$; describe a length as 0.62 meters; or locate 0.62 on a number line diagram.

> **Note.** This book will explore the standards that relate decimals to fractions, but not those standards focused solely on decimal computation.

IMPORTANT UNDERLYING IDEAS

> *Advantages of decimals over fractions.* Many students prefer decimals to fractions because decimals are easier to enter into calculators and perhaps because of the many life experiences in which students regularly encounter decimals, such as money situations.

Because students are used to thinking of decimals (e.g., 0.39 as a number of cents), it is not hard for them to think in hundredths. Helping students see that 1 penny is $\frac{1}{100}$ of a dollar (since 100 pennies make a dollar) should help student think of 0.39 as 39 hundredths.

One useful tool might be a hundredths grid filled with pennies, as shown on the next page.

Students can model various decimals on the grid to get a feel for what part of a whole each decimal of the form 0.☐☐ is, with ☐☐ representing any possible two digits for the decimal ☐☐ hundredths (e.g., 0.45, which is 45 hundredths, by using 45 pennies on the grid).

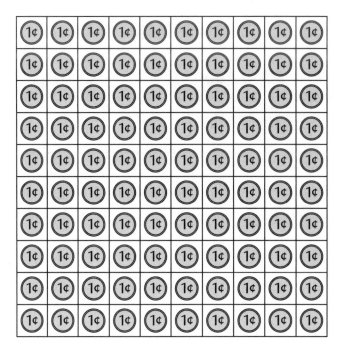

> ➤ **Representing tenths and hundredths simultaneously.** Students might notice that
> if they fill entire rows (or columns) of the 10 × 10 grid, they are representing both
> tenths and hundredths. For example, filling 4 rows of a 10 × 10 grid is a model for
> both 0.4 (four tenths) and 0.40 (forty hundredths).

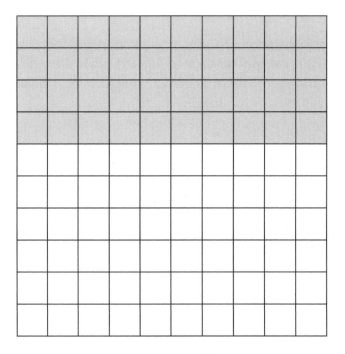

This type of understanding is critical when students are asked to calculate with decimals that don't all have the same number of digits to the right of the decimal point.

➤ **Relating the use of decimals to place value.** Deliberate attention must be given to helping students see that using a decimal is a way of extending the place value system to include numbers less than 1. Just as each familiar place value column heading is $\frac{1}{10}$ of the value of the one to its immediate left, tenths are to the right of ones and hundredths are to the right of tenths.

Thousands	Hundreds	Tens	Ones	Tenths	Hundredths

We must explain that the decimal point is placed between the ones and the tenths places in order to help us read the number properly (e.g., to distinguish 4 ones from 4 tenths).

Often students ask why there is no "oneths" place, and one can see why they might ask this. One way to help students is to emphasize that the decimal point is actually not in its own column; it is a "marker" that goes with the ones. The line of symmetry for the place value chart goes through the ones column and is not to the right of it.

It is because decimals are part of the place value system that we often use the convention of writing the whole number 0 before the decimal point for decimal values of less than 1, for example, 0.45 rather than .45. It is not something that would be obvious otherwise. It is not really wrong not to write the 0, rather it is simply a convention used in order to remind us that there are no ones, so the value is less than 1.

➤ **A decimal as a sum.** Students need to recognize that 0.42 is a way of writing 0.4 + 0.02, just as 123 is a way of writing 100 + 20 + 3. Since students know that $\frac{4}{10} = \frac{40}{100}$, they can add $\frac{40}{100}$ and $\frac{2}{100}$ to get $\frac{42}{100}$ to confirm why this makes sense. Alternately, students might color in 4 columns and 2 more squares in a hundredths grid and realize that 42 squares have been colored, but so has 4 tenths (4 columns or rows) and 2 more hundredths.

Because 0.42 is a bit more than 0.4, but not quite 0.5, students can learn to place 0.42 on a number line.

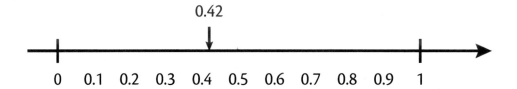

If the number line were a meter stick made up of 100 cm, it would be even easier—by counting 42 cm from 0, or just by finding the 42 cm tick on the meter stick. Students would see that, since 1 cm = 0.01 m, then 42 cm = 0.42 m.

Using the number line (or meter stick), students should realize that the decimal 0.☐5 is always halfway between two decimal tenths (with ☐ used here as a placeholder for "any number"). For example, 0.35 is halfway between 0.3 and 0.4. Students should also realize that decimals of the form 0.☐1 are just a little more than decimal tenths, for example, 0.71 is just a little more than 0.7, and decimals of the form 0.☐9 are just a little less than decimal tenths, for example, 0.39 is almost 0.4.

Decimals greater than 1 can also be thought of as sums. For example, 12.23 = 12 + 0.23 or 12 + 0.2 + 0.03 or 10 + 2 + 0.23, etc.

Good Questions to Ask

- *Ask students how they know that 0.4 < 1.*
- *Ask: A decimal hundredth is just a little more than 0.6. What might it be? What if it's just a little less? [This task requires use of the mathematical practice standard of reasoning abstractly and quantitatively.]*
- *Ask students how to write the decimal 0.53 as the sum of two fractions, first using the same denominator and then using different denominators. Observe whether they use $\frac{50}{100} + \frac{3}{100}$ or consider possibilities like $\frac{49}{100} + \frac{4}{100}$ for like denominators. Observe whether they realize they could use $\frac{5}{10} + \frac{3}{100}$ as a simple answer using different denominators.*

Comparing Decimals

Number and Operations—Fractions	CCSSM 4.NF
Understand decimal notation for fractions, and compare decimal fractions.	

7. Compare two decimals to hundredths by reasoning about their size. Recognize that comparisons are valid only when the two decimals refer to the same whole. Record the results of comparisons with the symbols >, =, or <, and justify the conclusions, e.g., by using a visual model.

IMPORTANT UNDERLYING IDEAS

➤ *Advantages of decimals over fractions.* One of the advantages for using decimals instead of fractions is to make comparisons easier. Students easily see that 0.67 > 0.60, but struggle more to see that $\frac{2}{3} > \frac{3}{5}$. This is because the use of decimals allows them to essentially use whole number thinking. It is also because the use of decimal hundredths in both cases has effectively provided a common denominator to the two fractions, namely 100, without doing any extra work.

Students might consider, though, instances when comparing fractions is just as easy as comparing decimals. For example, comparing $\frac{2}{5}$ and $\frac{3}{5}$ is just as easy as comparing 0.4 and 0.6.

➤ *Thinking of comparisons of decimals in terms of units.* Students should realize that 0.42 < 0.48 not just because 42 < 48, but because 42 hundredths < 48 hundredths (i.e., there are fewer copies of the same unit).

➤ *Common misconceptions when comparing decimals tenths to decimal hundredths.* A common misconception held by many students is that, for example, 0.4 < 0.19 because 4 < 19. The problem is that the units are different: The 4 is 4 tenths, but the 19 is 19 hundredths. Many students will understand this if the analogy is made to measurement units (e.g., 4 feet is a lot more than 19 inches, even though 19 is more than 4).

Another approach is to use a visual model. Students can compare 0.4 of a hundredths grid to 0.19 of the same size grid to see why 0.4 is more.

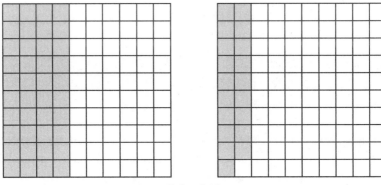

0.4 > 0.19

Although one can simply tell students to rewrite 0.4 as 0.40, it might be just as meaningful, if not more so, to explain that 0.19 is not even 2 tenths, so 4 tenths has to be more than an amount that is not even 2 tenths. Notice that the hundredths grid shows this. This type of thinking supports the mathematical practice standard of reasoning abstractly and constructing viable arguments.

Good Questions to Ask

- *Ask students what options they have to make the following true: 0.43 > 0.☐9. Have them explain their thinking.*
- *Ask students to draw pictures to show why 0.9 > 0.36.* [This is an example of the mathematical practice standard of using appropriate tools strategically.]
- *Ask students whether 0.1☐ < 0.29 no matter what value is in the blank, and why or why not.*
- *Ask students to fill in the blanks with any digits and then order the decimals from least to greatest:*

    0.☐☐   0.☐   0.☐1   0.4☐

Summary

Clearly Grade 4 work with fractions is a major step forward for students. They are introduced to decimals, to more significant work with improper fractions and mixed numbers (which are often more troubling to students than proper fractions), and to operations involving fractions, and they start to consolidate and broaden their understanding of what fractions mean.

For students to become successful with more complicated operational thinking in subsequent grades, 4th grade is critical for building a solid foundation.

GRADE 5

Representing Decimal Thousandths

Number and Operations in Base Ten	CCSSM 5.NBT
Understand the place value system.	

3. Read, write, and compare decimals to thousandths.
   a. Read and write decimals to thousandths using base-ten numerals, number names, and expanded form, e.g., $347.392 = 3 \times 100 + 4 \times 10 + 7 \times 1 + 3 \times \frac{1}{10} + 9 \times \frac{1}{100} + 2 \times \frac{1}{1000}$.

> **Note.** This book will explore the standards that relate decimals to fractions, but not standards focused solely on decimal computation. This is because the latter standards are really more about place value thinking than about fractional thinking.

IMPORTANT UNDERLYING IDEAS

> **Difficulties students experience with thousandths.** My research (Small, 2005) indicates that students have much more difficulty with decimal thousandths than with tenths or hundredths. Perhaps this is because there are so few instances in a child's life where decimal thousandths are seen. This is why it is important for students to see a variety of models, so that at least one of the models makes sense to them for visualizing what decimal thousandths actually are.

> **Models for thousandths.** One model that can support visualization of decimal thousandths is the thousandths grid. It is based on the hundredths grid, but each of the 100 cells is subdivided into 10 small rectangles, as two rows of five rectangles.

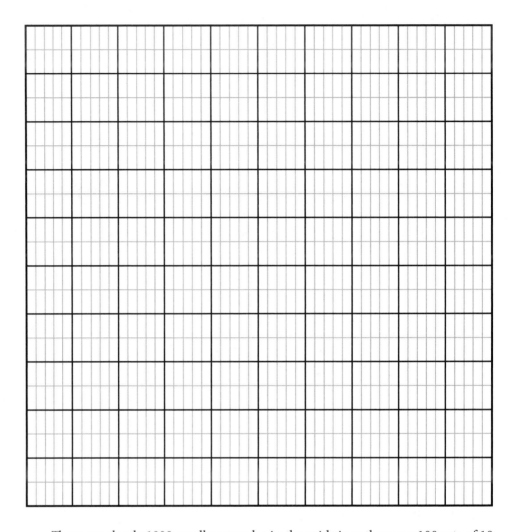

There are clearly 1000 small rectangles in the grid since there are 100 sets of 10 rectangles. It can also be seen that 0.01 (one hundredth) is made up of 10 thousandths, which is why 0.01 = 0.010, and that 0.1 (one tenth) is made up of 100 thousandths, which is why 0.1 = 0.100.

To model a decimal such as 0.124, one can shade 124 of the 1000 rectangles (as shown on the next page). An efficient way to do this is to use the notion that 0.124 = 0.1 + 0.02 + 0.004, coloring in one full row (or column) for the 0.1 part, two more of the 100 squares that make up the grid for the 0.02 part, and finally four more small rectangles for the 0.004 part.

This model also supports the notion that thousandths are very small relative to the whole.

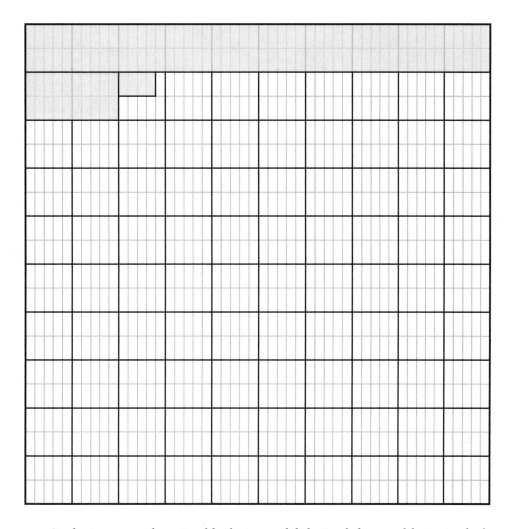

Students can use base-ten blocks to model decimal thousandths instead, although for many students, extensive earlier work with whole numbers using base-ten blocks can interfere. Students might have difficulty, for example, calling a large cube 1 instead of 1000, yet this is necessary in order to model thousandths. Blocks can be used to model thousandths if the large cube is worth 1, so the flat can be worth 0.1, the rod can be worth 0.01, and the small cube can be worth 0.001.

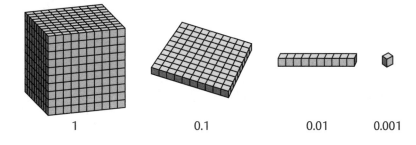

1   0.1   0.01   0.001

Using the blocks, 0.124 could be modeled with 124 small cubes, but could also be modeled using 1 flat (0.1) along with 2 rods (0.02) and 4 small cubes (0.004). A number like 3.124 could be modeled with 3 large blocks, 1 flat, 2 rods, and 4 small cubes.

Some students, but certainly not all, can handle more abstract concepts. For example, knowing that 1000 mm = 1 m, students could think of 0.124 as 124 mm compared to a meter stick. Or knowing that 1 km = 1000 m, they could think of 0.124 as 124 m relative to 1 km. Many other pairs of metric measures can be used (e.g., 1 mg = 0.001 g; 1 g = 0.001 kg; 1 mL = 0.001 L).

In a similar way, a student might think of a $10 bill as a unit, in which case a penny would be worth 0.001 units. Although this is mathematically correct and might help some students, it is very abstract for others.

> **The notion of precision when using decimals.** It is important for students to understand that we are likely to use thousandths only in situations where we wish to be very precise. For example, it is unlikely that we would measure someone's height in thousandths of a meter since that level of precision is not needed. However, in a very close high-level competition, like the Olympics, a competitor might win by only a few thousandths of a meter or thousandths of a second.

Good Questions to Ask

- Ask students why the model for 0.238 on a thousandths grid is almost but not quite $\frac{1}{4}$ of the grid.
- Ask students to explain why 2.314 is actually 2314 thousandths.
- Ask students to give several reasons why it makes sense that 10 thousandths make 1 hundredth. [They might refer to models, e.g., 10 small base-ten cubes is worth a rod, or they might use the notion that the fraction $\frac{10}{1000} = \frac{1}{100}$, or they might refer to the 10 small rectangles that make up each of the 100 squares on the thousandths grid.]

Comparing Decimals Involving Thousandths

Number and Operations in Base Ten	CCSM 5.NBT
Understand the place value system.	

3. Read, write, and compare decimals to thousandths.
   b. Compare two decimals to thousandths based on meanings of the digits in each place, using >, =, and < symbols to record the results of comparisons.

IMPORTANT UNDERLYING IDEAS

> *Comparing decimals using place value thinking.* One of the reasons that we sometimes use decimals rather than fractions is that they more closely mirror the kind of thinking that we do with whole numbers. This is as true for decimal comparisons as it is for decimal computation.

For example, just as we can say that 1342 > 1215 because, while both are slightly over 1000, one is more than 300 more whereas the other is not, we can also think that 0.235 > 0.146 because the first number is more than 2 tenths and the second is less than 2 tenths. Similarly, we could think that 0.235 > 0.218 since the first number is more than 23 hundredths and the second is not.

As with whole numbers, students can work from the left, one place value at a time, to decide which number is greater. Even when decimals have different levels of precision, this thinking is useful. For example, 1.2 > 1.119 since 1.2 is exactly 2 tenths greater than 1, while 1.119 is not even 2 tenths greater than 1 (the number of tenths is only 1, not 2).

Although some teachers suggest that students could rewrite 1.2 as 1.200 to make the comparison, this is not required when using this sort of place value thinking.

> *Comparing decimals by thinking in units.* As with simpler decimals, decimal thousandths can be compared by thinking of each decimal as a whole number of thousandths (or hundredths or tenths). For example, 3.121 > 3.115 since 3121 thousandths is more than 3115 thousandths.

If numbers have different numbers of decimal places, this sort of thinking can still be useful, as long as the same units are used. For example, 3.1 > 3.045 since 3100 thousandths is more than 3045 thousandths, or because 31 tenths is greater than 30.45 tenths. The first approach (using more of the smaller unit) is probably easier for more students than the second one (using decimals of the larger unit).

Good Questions to Ask

- Ask students: *A decimal thousandths number is just slightly more than 4.23. What might it be?*
- Ask students what values could go in the blanks to make this true? *1.2*☐☐ *< 1.*☐*39.*
- Ask students how they would explain why *3.12 is greater than 3.118, even though 312 is not greater than 3118.*
- Have students discuss the various models for thousandths that they have encountered, and ask them which they prefer and why.

Adding and Subtracting Fractions

Number and Operations—Fractions	CCSSM 5.NF
Use equivalent fractions as a strategy to add and subtract fractions.	

1. Add and subtract fractions with unlike denominators (including mixed numbers) by replacing given fractions with equivalent fractions in such a way as to produce an equivalent sum or difference of fractions with like denominators. For example, $\frac{2}{3} + \frac{5}{4} = \frac{8}{12} + \frac{15}{12} = \frac{23}{12}$. (In general, $\frac{a}{b} + \frac{c}{d} = \frac{ad+bc}{bd}$.)

2. Solve word problems involving addition and subtraction of fractions referring to the same whole, including cases of unlike denominators, e.g., by using visual fraction models or equations to represent the problem. Use benchmark fractions and number sense of fractions to estimate mentally and assess the reasonableness of answers. For example, recognize an incorrect result $\frac{2}{5} + \frac{1}{2} = \frac{3}{7}$, by observing that $\frac{3}{7} < \frac{1}{2}$.

IMPORTANT UNDERLYING IDEAS

> **Beginning with the concrete.** Students' first experiences with adding fractions with unlike denominators should be concrete or pictorial, rather than symbolic. For example, students could add $\frac{1}{2} + \frac{1}{3}$ using pattern blocks or fraction strips without actually getting the common denominator.

   If students are familiar with the notion that a hexagon might represent the whole, in which case the trapezoid represents $\frac{1}{2}$, the parallelogram $\frac{1}{3}$, and the triangle $\frac{1}{6}$, then they see that $\frac{1}{2} + \frac{1}{3}$ occupies $\frac{1}{6}$ less than the whole hexagon, so the sum must be $\frac{5}{6}$.

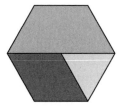

   Or they might place 3 and 2 triangle sixths, respectively, on the trapezoid and parallelogram to see why the result is 5 sixths.

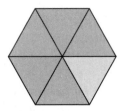

Students might also use fraction strips. They could add $\frac{1}{2}$ and $\frac{1}{3}$ by placing those strips side by side, searching for a strip of the same total length, in this case $\frac{5}{6}$.

$\frac{1}{2}$			$\frac{1}{3}$	
$\frac{1}{6}$	$\frac{1}{6}$	$\frac{1}{6}$	$\frac{1}{6}$	$\frac{1}{6}$

Both of these models indirectly show how $\frac{1}{2}$ and $\frac{1}{3}$ are renamed as $\frac{3}{6}$ and $\frac{2}{6}$, respectively, to see where the $\frac{5}{6}$ comes from.

These same models can be used for subtracting. This time, it makes sense to think of subtracting in terms of how much more one number is than the other, or, in other words, what must be added to the smaller amount to get to the greater one. For example, $\frac{1}{2} - \frac{1}{3}$ can be shown with pattern blocks by modeling $\frac{1}{3}$ (the dark gray parallelogram below) and figuring out what to add to it make a $\frac{1}{2}$.

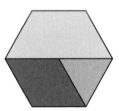

The added piece is the triangle, which is $\frac{1}{6}$ of the whole hexagon, so $\frac{1}{2} - \frac{1}{3} = \frac{1}{6}$. The same concept can be modeled with the fraction strips. The $\frac{1}{6}$ piece must be added to the $\frac{1}{3}$ piece to match the $\frac{1}{2}$ piece.

$\frac{1}{2}$	
$\frac{1}{3}$	$\frac{1}{6}$

> ➤ *A grid model for adding fractions.* Although fraction strips and pattern blocks
are useful for adding fractions, the grid model, also simple and useful, leads most
readily to the standard algorithm for adding fractions: $\frac{a}{b} + \frac{c}{d} = \frac{ad+bc}{bd}$.

For example, if students were adding $\frac{2}{5}$ to $\frac{1}{3}$, they would want a model where
it is easy to show both fifths and thirds. An ideal model is a 3 × 5 grid. On the grid
below, the white counters cover $\frac{2}{5}$ of the grid, since 2 out of the 5 columns are
filled. The gray counters cover $\frac{1}{3}$ of the grid since 1 out of the 3 rows is filled.

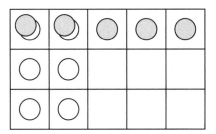

Students will see that only 9 cells are filled, but will realize something feels wrong
if a cell has 2 counters. After moving the counters so that there is only 1 counter
per cell, it is clear that $\frac{2}{5} + \frac{1}{3}$ fills $\frac{11}{15}$ of the grid, so the sum is $\frac{11}{15}$.

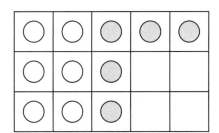

Notice that students have, without realizing it, renamed $\frac{2}{5}$ as $\frac{6}{15}$ and $\frac{1}{3}$ as $\frac{5}{15}$ in
order to add them.

Should the sum be greater than 1, two grids might be needed, but students
need to be reminded that the cell size is based on the number of divisions in one
whole. For example, $\frac{2}{3} + \frac{3}{5}$ would look like this initially.

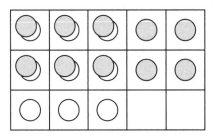

Then, when duplicates are moved, students will see that the total fills $1\frac{4}{15}$ grids.

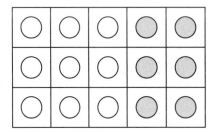 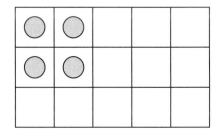

Some students will not feel the need to move duplicates. They would simply recognize that each counter represents $\frac{1}{15}$ and see that there are 10 gray counters and 9 white counters, so there are 19 counters, for a total of $\frac{19}{15}$.

Different grid sizes are possible. If, for example, students were adding denominators where one was a multiple of the other (e.g., 4ths and 8ths), they could either use a 4 × 8 grid, in which it is simple to show eighths as well as fourths, or they could use a smaller grid (e.g., a 4 × 2 grid), wherein they fill one of the 4 rows to show $\frac{1}{4}$ and 1 cell, rather than 1 column, to show $\frac{1}{8}$.

In these two cases, $\frac{3}{4} + \frac{1}{8}$ is seen as either $\frac{28}{32}$ or $\frac{7}{8}$. Both answers are correct.

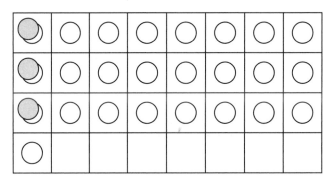 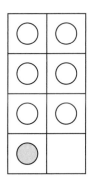

> **A grid model for subtracting fractions.** To subtract with grids, a take-away meaning of subtraction could be used. For example, $\frac{2}{3} - \frac{1}{4}$ would be modeled by creating a grid, such as a 3 × 4 grid, where it is easy to show both thirds and fourths.
>
> $\frac{2}{3}$ of the grid is filled by filling 2 of the 3 rows. Then counters that fill $\frac{1}{4}$ of the grid (not $\frac{1}{4}$ of the counters present, but $\frac{1}{4}$ of the grid) would be removed by first moving 1 of the counters so that 1 of the 4 columns is full and then that amount is removed.

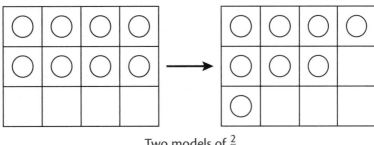

Two models of $\frac{2}{3}$

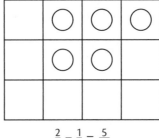

$\frac{2}{3} - \frac{1}{4} = \frac{5}{12}$

The reason that we remove $\frac{1}{4}$ of the full grid, and not $\frac{1}{4}$ of the counters present is because it is necessary to subtract $\frac{1}{4}$ from the same whole that $\frac{2}{3}$ is already a part of. If, instead we were to remove $\frac{1}{4}$ of the total counters present, then we would actually be subtracting $\frac{1}{4} \times \frac{2}{3}$ from $\frac{2}{3}$, rather than $\frac{1}{4}$ from $\frac{2}{3}$.

> *Adding or subtracting fractions by appealing to whole-number thinking.* Many older children regularly convert fractions to percents in order to compare or compute with them. What they are essentially doing is indicating that they would rather work with whole numbers. For example, to add $\frac{2}{5} + \frac{1}{4}$ by adding 40% and 25% to get 65% (or $\frac{65}{100}$), they are simply recognizing that $\frac{2}{5}$ of 100 + $\frac{1}{4}$ of 100 is some fraction of 100. If they know what part of 100 the sum is, then they've answered the question.

But they don't only have to work with 100. For example, to add $\frac{2}{5} + \frac{1}{4}$, they could have chosen to work with 20. $\frac{2}{5}$ of 20 + $\frac{1}{4}$ of 20 is some fraction of 20. That fraction is also the answer to $\frac{2}{5} + \frac{1}{4}$.

Since $\frac{2}{5}$ of 20 is 8 and $\frac{1}{4}$ of 20 is 5 and 8 + 5 = 13, the sum must be 13 out of 20 (which is $\frac{13}{20}$ and, of course, also $\frac{65}{100}$). Notice that 20 makes sense to use in this situation because it is relatively easy to calculate both fifths and fourths of 20. This connects closely to the grid model in the previous section. Thinking in this way is an example of the mathematical practice standard of reasoning abstractly and quantitatively.

It is equally true that $\frac{2}{5}$ of 30 and $\frac{1}{4}$ of 30 can be calculated to determine $\frac{2}{5} + \frac{1}{4}$, but it's simply more difficult to calculate. In this case, the sum would be $12 + 7\frac{1}{2}$, which is

$$\frac{19\frac{1}{2}}{30}.$$

Although this solution is awkward, the result is correct and could be renamed as $\frac{39}{60}$ if that were preferred.

Building a connection to whole numbers is also possible for subtraction. To subtract $\frac{2}{5} - \frac{1}{4}$, a student might use any of these strategies:

$\frac{2}{5}$ of 100 is 40 and $\frac{1}{4}$ of 100 is 25.

$40 - 25 = 15$

Since this is $\frac{15}{100}$, $\frac{2}{5} - \frac{1}{4} = \frac{15}{100}$.

$\frac{2}{5}$ of 40 is 16 and $\frac{1}{4}$ of 40 is 10.

$16 - 10 = 6$

Since this is $\frac{6}{40}$, $\frac{2}{5} - \frac{1}{4} = \frac{6}{40}$.

$\frac{2}{5}$ of 20 is 8 and $\frac{1}{4}$ of 20 is 5

$8 - 5 = 3$

Since this is $\frac{3}{20}$, $\frac{2}{5} - \frac{1}{4} = \frac{3}{20}$.

These strategies focus on thinking of fractions as parts of sets.

➤ *Explaining why we use common denominators.* To help students understand why we use equivalent fractions with common denominators to add or subtract fractions, it helps to relate back to measurement concepts. Students can see that it is hard to know how much 3 ft + 2 in is without converting either the feet to inches or the inches to feet. Similarly, it's hard to know how much 3 fifths + 2 eighths is. However, if it had been 3 fifths + 2 fifths, we would know it is a total of 5 fifths, even without visualizing the model. So, rather than adding fifths and eighths, it helps if the fractions are named with the same unit (e.g., fortieths); we know that 24 fortieths added to 10 fortieths must be 34 fortieths, without even seeing the amounts.

At some points, students will realize that if the two fractions are $\frac{a}{b}$ and $\frac{c}{d}$, one of the ways to get a common denominator is to rename the fractions as $\frac{ad}{bd}$ and $\frac{bc}{bd}$. Since these equivalents have the same denominator, the numerators can be added.

$$\frac{a}{b} + \frac{c}{d} = \frac{ad}{bd} + \frac{bc}{bd} = \frac{ad+bc}{bd}$$

Showing the "motions" of how to cross-multiply and add should not be a focus of instruction at this level, but it still might be noticed by students.

> **Which common denominator to use.** Students should understand why one possible common denominator is the product of the two original denominators. For example, in calculating $\frac{2}{5} - \frac{1}{3}$, a common denominator is 15 (5 × 3). This is because if both terms of the first fraction are multiplied by the second denominator and both terms of the second fraction are multiplied by the first denominator, equivalents are produced, but in each case the new denominator is the product of the two original denominators.

Students should realize that, although the above approach is always correct, simpler approaches can sometimes be used. For example, when adding $\frac{1}{8} + \frac{3}{16}$, students could rename the fractions as $\frac{16}{128}$ and $\frac{24}{128}$, but it is much simpler to leave $\frac{3}{16}$ alone and rename $\frac{1}{8}$ as $\frac{2}{16}$. Students can be encouraged to look at the two denominators and determine the least possible number that is a multiple of both (i.e., the least common multiple). But it is never wrong to use a common denominator that is not the lowest possible.

> **Estimating sums and differences.** Although it is sometimes hard to estimate fraction sums and differences, students should be encouraged to try. They might reason in ways similar to those described in these examples:

$\frac{2}{3} + \frac{3}{4}$	$\frac{3}{4}$ is not that much more than $\frac{2}{3}$, so the sum should be a bit more than 2 groups of $\frac{2}{3}$, which is $\frac{4}{3}$. **OR** The sum is more than $\frac{1}{2} + \frac{1}{2}$, which is 1, but less than 1 + 1, which is 2.
$\frac{1}{5} + \frac{2}{3}$	$\frac{1}{5}$ is less than $\frac{1}{3}$. Since $\frac{1}{3} + \frac{2}{3}$ is 1, the sum should be less than 1, but more than $\frac{2}{3}$.
$\frac{5}{6} - \frac{1}{4}$	$\frac{1}{4}$ is a bit more than $\frac{1}{6}$, so the difference should be a bit less than $\frac{5}{6} - \frac{1}{6}$, or $\frac{4}{6}$. [Subtracting more, $\frac{1}{4}$ instead of $\frac{1}{6}$, leaves less.] **OR** $\frac{5}{6}$ is a little more than $\frac{3}{4}$, so the difference should be a bit more than $\frac{3}{4} - \frac{1}{4}$, or $\frac{1}{2}$.
$\frac{7}{8} - \frac{1}{10}$	$\frac{1}{10}$ is so little, the difference should be not much less than $\frac{7}{8}$.

➤ **Adding mixed numbers.** Although students might rename mixed numbers as improper fractions in order to add them, by using the rules for adding fractions described above, students can estimate better if they leave the mixed numbers in that form. For example, for $1\frac{2}{3} + 3\frac{1}{4}$, the sum is about $1 + 3 + 1$ (the last 1 being an estimate for $\frac{2}{3} + \frac{1}{4}$), or 5. To calculate, the students add the 1 and 3 to get 4, and add $\frac{2}{3}$ and $\frac{1}{4}$ using one of the strategies above to get $\frac{11}{12}$. The exact sum is therefore $4 + \frac{11}{12}$ or, based on their knowledge of mixed numbers, $4\frac{11}{12}$.

Had the fraction sum been greater than 1, students would rename the fraction-part sum as a mixed number and add it to the whole-number sum. For example, for $1\frac{2}{3} + 3\frac{3}{4}$, they would add $1 + 3$ to get 4 and add $\frac{2}{3} + \frac{3}{4}$ to get $\frac{17}{12}$, or $1\frac{5}{12}$. The sum is therefore $4 + 1\frac{5}{12}$, which is $5\frac{5}{12}$.

Although it is possible to model the addition of mixed numbers concretely, it tends to be awkward, and it is not appropriate to be working with mixed numbers until students are facile with adding simple fractions.

➤ **Subtracting mixed numbers.** As with addition, mixed numbers can be renamed as improper fractions and then subtracted using what students already know about subtracting fractions. But students should be encouraged to see the value in retaining the mixed number form so that estimates of the answers are easier to make.

For example, for $3\frac{1}{2} - 1\frac{1}{8}$, the student could estimate that this is about $3\frac{1}{2} - 1 = 2\frac{1}{2}$. To get an exact answer, they could separately subtract $3 - 1 = 2$ and $\frac{1}{2} - \frac{1}{8} = \frac{3}{8}$ to get an answer of 2 and $\frac{3}{8}$, or $2\frac{3}{8}$. [Sometimes students make the mistake of subtracting the $\frac{3}{8}$ from the 2, rather than adding the two results; they are focused on doing a subtraction problem, so they subtract. But they should realize that they are taking away the $1\frac{1}{8}$, so they are left with 2 wholes and also $\frac{3}{8}$ of a whole.]

If the fractional part of the mixed number being subtracted is greater than the fractional part of the greater mixed number, this strategy must be modified. In that case, there are several alternate approaches.

One strategy is to think like this: For $2\frac{3}{8} - 1\frac{3}{4}$, we begin with 2 wholes and $\frac{3}{8}$ more of another. If we want to subtract 1 whole, there is no problem. But instead of taking the $\frac{3}{4}$ part from the $\frac{3}{8}$, it can be taken from the remaining whole.

The student thinks: $1 - \frac{3}{4} = \frac{4}{4} - \frac{3}{4} = \frac{1}{4}$. There is still the $\frac{3}{8}$ that has not been used, so what is left is $\frac{1}{4} + \frac{3}{8}$, which is $\frac{5}{8}$.

The steps can be summarized this way:

1. subtract the whole part of the lesser number from the whole part of the greater number

2. subtract the fraction being subtracted from one of the wholes that are left from step 1

3. add the resulting fraction from step 2 to the resulting whole number from step 1

4. add the fraction attached to the greater number

Another strategy is to rename the greater number by taking one of the wholes and renaming it as a convenient fraction.

For $2\frac{3}{8} - 1\frac{3}{4}$, we begin with 2 wholes and $\frac{3}{8}$ more of another. One can rename this problem as $1\frac{11}{8} - 1\frac{3}{4}$, and then proceed. Some students will prefer this strategy over the previous one; others will prefer the former approach.

Although it is certainly possible to model the subtraction of mixed numbers concretely, it tends to be awkward, and, as with addition, it is not appropriate to be working with mixed numbers until students are facile with subtracting simple fractions.

> *Meanings of subtraction when working with fractions.* When working with real-world problems involving the addition of fractions, it is virtually always a case of combining. But subtraction involves different situations and strategies. Students need to meet each of these situations and benefit from modeling the problem in a manner consistent with the meaning inherent in the problem being solved.

For example, if the problem asked how many cups of sugar were left if there were $2\frac{2}{3}$ cups and someone used $1\frac{1}{4}$ cups, students might separately subtract the whole numbers and the fractions, thinking of "taking away."

If the problem asked how many more cups of sugar are needed if someone has $1\frac{1}{4}$ cups and needs $2\frac{1}{3}$ cups, adding up might make sense.

If the problem asked how many more cups of flour than sugar are used if someone uses $2\frac{2}{3}$ cups of flour and $1\frac{3}{4}$ cups of sugar, the student might add up or might model both fractions to see how much more one is than the other.

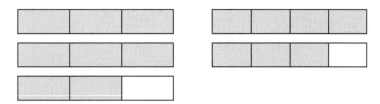

The student can see there is $\frac{2}{3}$ more flour than sugar shown in the bottom row and $\frac{1}{4}$ more flour in the middle row, so the total extra flour is calculated as $\frac{2}{3} + \frac{1}{4} = \frac{11}{12}$ of a cup.

> *Common misconceptions about adding fractions.* Because students have greater comfort with whole numbers than they do with fractions, when they see a calculation

such as $\frac{2}{3} + \frac{1}{4}$, it is a natural error for them to add numerators and add denominators to get $\frac{3}{7}$. Hopefully, if students have been encouraged to estimate, they would realize that it is impossible to start with an addend of more than $\frac{1}{2}$ (which $\frac{2}{3}$ is) and end up with a result that is less than $\frac{1}{2}$ (which $\frac{3}{7}$ is). (In fact, students might be led to discover that the fraction that is created by adding numerators and denominators always falls between the two original fractions.) When students make these kinds of natural errors, estimation becomes a very powerful tool for catching these errors.

Good Questions to Ask

- *Ask students to provide four different pairs of fractions that they know will add to a result close to $\frac{3}{4}$ without having to actually do the addition. They should explain how they estimated.* [Possible solutions include $\frac{2}{10} + \frac{5}{10}$, which students might think of by visualizing a tenths grid; $\frac{1}{3} + \frac{2}{4}$, since $\frac{1}{4} + \frac{2}{4}$ would be $\frac{3}{4}$, and $\frac{1}{3}$ is close to $\frac{1}{4}$; $\frac{1}{3} + \frac{3}{8}$, since $\frac{3}{8} + \frac{3}{8}$ is $\frac{3}{4}$, and $\frac{1}{3}$ is close to $\frac{3}{8}$. This task supports the mathematical practice standard of reasoning abstractly and quantitatively.]
- *Tell students that someone has added two fractions and the sum is $\frac{12}{10}$. Ask what the original denominators might have been and how they know.* [Although expected answers are 10 and 10, 10 and 5, 10 and 2, or 10 and 1, students could think 10 and 3 if they chose to use $\frac{3}{3} + \frac{2}{10}$.]
- *Ask students to create a real-life problem that would be solved by calculating $\frac{2}{3} - \frac{3}{5}$. Ask them to explain why the problem is a subtraction one.*
- *Ask students to create a pair of fractions with different denominators whose sum is the same as the difference of another pair of fractions with different denominators. Ask them to explain their process.* [An example might be $\frac{1}{2} + \frac{3}{8}$ and $\frac{2}{2} - \frac{1}{8}$.]
- *Tell students that two fractions, both less than 1, sum to almost $1\frac{2}{3}$. Ask what the fractions might be. Observe whether students realize that one possibility is any fraction close to but less than 1 (e.g., $\frac{9}{10}$) added to $\frac{2}{3}$, but that there are many other possibilities as well.*
- *Ask students to place the digits 2, 3, 4, 5, 8, and 9 into the operation $\square\frac{\square}{\square} - \square\frac{\square}{\square}$ in order to create a difference between 1 and 2.*

Interpreting Fractions as an Implied Division

Number and Operations—Fractions	CCSSM 5.NF

Apply and extend previous understandings of multiplication and division to multiply and divide fractions.

3. Interpret a fraction as division of the numerator by the denominator ($\frac{a}{b} = a \div b$). Solve word problems involving division of whole numbers leading to answers in the form of fractions or mixed numbers, e.g., by using visual fraction models or equations to represent the problem. For example, interpret $\frac{3}{4}$ as the result of dividing 3 by 4, noting that $\frac{3}{4}$ multiplied by 4 equals 3, and that when 3 wholes are shared equally among 4 people each person has a share of size $\frac{3}{4}$. If 9 people want to share a 50-pound sack of rice equally by weight, how many pounds of rice should each person get? Between what two whole numbers does your answer lie?

IMPORTANT UNDERLYING IDEAS

> *Interpreting $\frac{1}{b}$ as $1 \div b$.* It is important for students to learn that another meaning for the fraction $\frac{a}{b}$ is $a \div b$. This is usually simple for students to recognize when the fraction has a numerator of 1. One interpretation of division is sharing; for example, $10 \div 2$ tells the share size if 10 is divided into 2 equal groups. Therefore $1 \div 3$ should be the share size when 1 whole is divided into 3 equal parts, and that is exactly what we mean by $\frac{1}{3}$. This concept when the numerator is something other than 1 requires more thought.

> *Interpreting improper fractions as implied division.* Another meaning of division is counting how many equal groups of a certain size can be created using a given amount. For example, $8 \div 2$ asks how many groups of 2 are in 8. When renaming improper fractions as mixed numbers, this meaning of division makes the most sense to use.

For example, $\frac{12}{3} = 4$ because it takes 3 thirds to make a whole and we divide 12 by 3 to figure out how many groups of 3 are in 12. That tells us how many wholes there are: for example, $\frac{12}{5} = 2\frac{2}{5}$ because $12 \div 5 = 2$ with a remainder of 2. The 2 sets of 5 fifths make the 2 wholes. The remainder of 2 represents $\frac{2}{5}$ of another group of 5.

In fact, some researchers believe that modeling fractions as division is actually a good way to introduce the concept of fractions (Teaching and Learning Research Programme, 2006).

➤ *Interpreting proper fractions with a numerator other than 1 as implied division.* It is usually most difficult for students to understand why a fraction like $\frac{2}{3}$ is 2 ÷ 3. They generally think of $\frac{2}{3}$ as 2 sets of $\frac{1}{3}$, not as 2 wholes shared among 3 (the sharing meaning of division), nor as how many 3s are in 2 (the counting-how-many-groups meaning of division).

Using the first meaning, students might realize that if there are 2 items, each 1 could be shared into 3 equal parts, and each person gets 1 part from each item.

First person's share	Second person's share	Third person's share

First person's share	Second person's share	Third person's share

Each share is $\frac{1}{3}$ of a whole, so each person gets $\frac{2}{3}$ of a whole in total.

This approach to sharing can be generalized to any fraction. For example, if 5 is divided by 6, a person gets $\frac{1}{6}$ of each of the 5 items. The share is 5 one sixths, which is $\frac{5}{6}$ of one whole.

Using the second meaning of division, students might observe that 2 is $\frac{2}{3}$ of a single group of 3, so the number of groups of 3 in 2 is $\frac{2}{3}$ of 1 group, or $\frac{2}{3}$.

Good Questions to Ask

- *Ask students to draw pictures or build models to show each:*
    - *why $\frac{1}{3}$ = 1 ÷ 3*   ◆ *why $\frac{10}{3}$ = 10 ÷ 3*   ◆ *why $\frac{3}{10}$ = 3 ÷ 10*
  In each situation, ask students to describe what it is about the picture or model that represents division.
- *Tell students that there are 3 sandwiches. Ask them to choose a number of people greater than 3 to share the sandwiches equally and tell what part of a sandwich each gets.* [*Make sure to discuss why some students will think that using 6, 9, 12, . . . sharers is a bit easier, since each time they get a simple unit fraction (a fraction with a numerator of 1) for an answer.*]
- *Ask students to explain why some adults write $\frac{4}{5}$ when they mean 4 ÷ 5.*

Multiplying Fractions

Number and Operations—Fractions	CCSSM 5.NF

Apply and extend previous understandings of multiplication and division to multiply and divide fractions.

4. Apply and extend previous understandings of multiplication to multiply a fraction or whole number by a fraction.
   a. Interpret the product $\frac{a}{b} \times q$ as a parts of a partition of q into b equal parts; equivalently, as the result of a sequence of operations $a \times q \div b$. For example, use a visual fraction model to show $\frac{2}{3} \times 4 = \frac{8}{3}$, and create a story context for this equation. Do the same with $\frac{2}{3} \times \frac{4}{5} = \frac{8}{15}$. (In general, $\frac{a}{b} \times \frac{c}{d} = \frac{ac}{bd}$.)
   b. Find the area of a rectangle with fractional side lengths by tiling it with unit squares of the appropriate unit fraction side lengths, and show that the area is the same as would be found by multiplying the side lengths. Multiply fractional side lengths to find areas of rectangles, and represent fraction products as rectangular areas.

5. Interpret multiplication as scaling (resizing), by:
   a. Comparing the size of a product to the size of one factor on the basis of the size of the other factor, without performing the indicated multiplication.
   b. Explaining why multiplying a given number by a fraction greater than 1 results in a product greater than the given number (recognizing multiplication by whole numbers greater than 1 as a familiar case); explaining why multiplying a given number by a fraction less than 1 results in a product smaller than the given number; and relating the principle of fraction equivalence $\frac{a}{b} = \frac{n \times a}{n \times b}$ to the effect of multiplying $\frac{a}{b}$ by 1.

6. Solve real world problems involving multiplication of fractions and mixed numbers, e.g., by using visual fraction models or equations to represent the problem.

IMPORTANT UNDERLYING IDEAS

> *The difference between $\frac{a}{b} \times c$ and $c \times \frac{a}{b}$.* When we write $\frac{2}{3} \times 8$, for example, we want students to interpret this to mean $\frac{2}{3}$ of 8. This is to be consistent with whole number multiplication. For example, 4×8 means 4 groups of 8, so $\frac{2}{3} \times 8$ should mean $\frac{2}{3}$ of a group of 8, which is the same as $\frac{2}{3}$ of 8.

In 4th grade, students learned that $5 \times \frac{2}{3} = \frac{10}{3}$. Although we want students to realize that multiplication is commutative, that the order does not matter, the meanings of $5 \times \frac{2}{3}$ and $\frac{2}{3} \times 5$ are somewhat different. In the first instance, we are modeling 5 sets of $\frac{2}{3}$. On the other hand, $\frac{2}{3} \times 5$ would be represented by modeling 5 wholes and taking $\frac{2}{3}$ of that entire amount.

In the number line model shown below, the distance from 0 to 5 is cut into 3 equal parts, and we read the number at the end of the second part to tell what $\frac{2}{3}$ of 5 is.

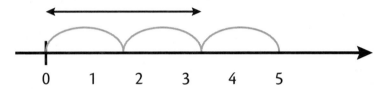

From this model, the result is clearly slightly more than 3, so $\frac{10}{3}$ seems reasonable, although the fact that it is $\frac{10}{3}$ is not completely obvious.

If more divisions between the whole numbers had been shown, it would have been easier to be more accurate. Since there are 15 small sections, it is clear that each third encompasses 5 of those sections. Since each small section is $\frac{1}{3}$, the end of the segment marking $\frac{2}{3}$ of 5 is $\frac{10}{3}$.

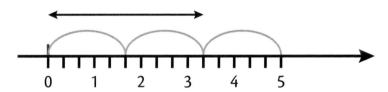

Another possible model for $\frac{2}{3}$ of 5 might look like this:

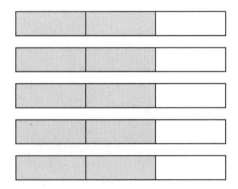

Clearly the total is $\frac{10}{3}$ since there are 5×2 thirds, which is also $5 \times 2 \div 3$.

More generally, $\frac{a}{b} \times c$ is $a \times c$ sets of $\frac{1}{b}$, or $\frac{a \times c}{b}$. Rather than just giving a rule, students should generalize this notion using models.

➤ **Interpreting $\frac{a}{b} \times b$ or $\frac{a}{b} \times a$ multiple of b.** Although students can calculate $\frac{3}{4} \times 4$ as $\frac{12}{4} = 3$ or $\frac{2}{5} \times 5$ as $\frac{10}{5} = 2$, they might "shortcut" this process.

$\frac{3}{4}$ of an amount indicates that we only want 3 out of its 4 equal parts. So $\frac{3}{4}$ of 4 (4 ones) is clearly 3. That means $\frac{3}{4} \times 4 = 3$.

Similarly, $\frac{2}{5}$ of 5 ones is clearly 2 ones. That means $\frac{2}{5} \times 5 = 2$.

Although this used to be called canceling, $\frac{2}{\cancel{5}} \times \cancel{5}$, canceling is not a particularly meaningful word and can lead to misconceptions. For example, we do not want students to think that $\frac{3}{5} \times 15 = 31$, since they can cross out the 5s.

In the case where we are calculating $\frac{2}{3} \times 6$ (instead of $\frac{2}{3} \times 3$), the result is 2×2, since 6 is two 3s. Taking $\frac{2}{3}$ of each set of 3 results in $2 \times 2 = 4$.

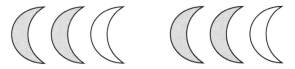

➤ **Interpreting multiplication of fractions using partitioning.** Just as the expression $\frac{2}{5} \times 10$ means $\frac{2}{5}$ of 10, the expression $\frac{2}{5} \times \frac{3}{4}$ means $\frac{2}{5}$ of $\frac{3}{4}$.

To calculate that product using fraction strips, the student could model $\frac{3}{4}$ and then separately take $\frac{2}{5}$ of each of the three fourths.

The student sees that there are 3×2 shaded pieces out of 5×4 pieces, or $\frac{6}{20}$.

Some students will struggle with why $\frac{2}{5}$ of the last section is not included. The emphasis is on the fact that doing that would actually be taking $\frac{2}{5}$ of the whole and not just $\frac{2}{5}$ of $\frac{3}{4}$.

Other students will wonder why $\frac{2}{5}$ of each $\frac{1}{4}$ section is shaded rather than $\frac{2}{5}$ of the full $\frac{3}{4}$. In fact $\frac{2}{5}$ of the full $\frac{3}{4}$ could be represented, as shown below. Notice that again $\frac{3}{4}$ is renamed as $\frac{15}{20}$, so that it is easier to divide the amount into five pieces. The $\frac{15}{20}$ is divided into 5 sections of $\frac{3}{20}$ and the first two sections are counted.

Students should be helped to see that whenever we multiply $\frac{a}{b} \times \frac{c}{d}$, we model $\frac{c}{d}$, so there are c colored sections out of d total sections. If we then divide each of the d sections into b parts, there are a total of $b \times d$ parts. In each situation, only a of the b parts are colored, so there are a total of $c \times a$ parts colored out of $b \times d$ parts.

> *Interpreting multiplication as a way to describe rectangle areas.* Just as students know that 3×4 is the area of a rectangle that is 3 units $\times$ 4 units, students can interpret $\frac{2}{3} \times \frac{3}{5}$ as the area of a rectangle that is $\frac{2}{3}$ of a unit by $\frac{3}{5}$ of a unit.

They can begin with a 1 unit $\times$ 1 unit square and subdivide it to make it easy to see $\frac{2}{3}$ and $\frac{3}{5}$ as the length and width.

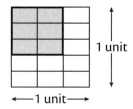

Since the area of the whole square is 1, the area of the shaded rectangle, which is $\frac{2}{3}$ unit $\times$ $\frac{3}{5}$ unit, is $\frac{6}{15}$ unit^2.

Notice that there are 2×3 sections colored, since one numerator was 2 and the other was 3. Notice, too, there are 3×5 sections in total since the two denominators were 3 and 5.

This same type of model can be used even if one of the fractions is greater than 1. For example, this model shows that $\frac{3}{5} \times \frac{5}{3} = \frac{15}{15}$. What has to be emphasized, though, is that each small rectangle is worth $\frac{1}{15}$, not $\frac{1}{30}$, even though there are

30 rectangles in the drawing. That is because 1 whole is made up of only 15 rectangles.

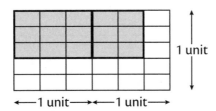

At this point, the concept that multiplying a fraction by $\frac{n}{n}$ results in an equivalent fraction might be discussed. If, for example, $\frac{2}{3}$ is multiplied by $\frac{3}{3}$, there is a rectangle with a length of $\frac{2}{3}$ and a width of $\frac{3}{3}$, or 1. Clearly the area is $\frac{2}{3}$ of 1 square unit, even though it is also $\frac{6}{9}$ of 1.

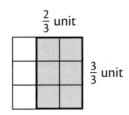

➤ **Interpreting multiplication as scaling.** When we say that 1 object is 4 times as much as another, we are thinking of the smaller object as 1 unit and the larger as 4 of those units. For example, the white rectangle is 4 times as long as the gray one since it would take 4 gray units to make up the white.

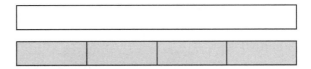

It is as if we created an enlarged version of the gray rectangle in a scale diagram, where 1 white on the diagram is modeled to represent 1 gray in terms of actual length.

In a similar way, one can think of multiplying by $\frac{2}{3}$ as scaling a length to $\frac{2}{3}$ of its original. An original length (the gray) would be shown as a length $\frac{2}{3}$ as long (the white).

> **Relative sizes of products.** To help students estimate products of fractions, students should think about the effect of multiplying by various types of fractions. For example, multiplying a number by $\frac{3}{2}$ results in all of the original number plus another half of it, which is more than the original amount. On the other hand, multiplying by $\frac{2}{3}$ results in only part of the original value.

More generally, students should realize that multiplying by any proper fraction results in less than the starting amount, but multiplying by any improper fraction results in more than the starting amount. Attention to this type of generalization builds on the mathematical practice standard of looking for and making use of structure.

> **Multiplying mixed numbers.** One approach to multiplying mixed numbers is to rename them as improper fractions and multiply using the approaches students have already learned.

Another approach is to use the area model and do 4 simple multiplications, adding the results. For example, for $1\frac{2}{3} \times 2\frac{1}{5}$

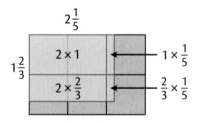

The total is $2 + \frac{4}{3} + \frac{1}{5} + \frac{2}{15}$. This can be summed as $2 + \frac{25}{15} = 3\frac{10}{15}$.

Although the area model does appear to some students as more work, it helps students better estimate the answer, in this case as about 4.

> **Recognizing multiplication of fraction situations.** Students should notice a variety of contexts for multiplication with fractions that make sense. These include:

- taking part of something (e.g., There were $3\frac{1}{2}$ cups of punch, and $\frac{2}{3}$ of it was used. How much was left?)
- scaling (e.g., On a scale diagram, each length is represented as $\frac{1}{12}$ of its actual length. How long would a 54" table be on the diagram?)
- calculating area (e.g., A carpet is 3'5" long and 3'1" wide. What is its area in square feet? To determine this, students might rewrite the dimensions as $3\frac{5}{12}$ ft long and $3\frac{1}{12}$ ft wide.)

Good Questions to Ask

- *Ask students to draw a picture to show that $3 \times \frac{2}{5}$ has the same value as $2 \times \frac{3}{5}$. Then ask if it is always possible to switch the numerator and the whole number multiplier to result in the same value. Have students justify their reasoning to use the mathematical practice standard of constructing viable arguments.*
- *Ask students to name two fractions to multiply to result in each situation:*
    - *the product is less than both fractions*
    - *the product is greater than both fractions*
    - *the product is greater than one of the fractions, but less than the other*

[In the first case, both fractions are less than 1; in the second case, they are both greater than 1; in the third case, one is less than 1 and one is greater than 1. This question goes directly to a common student misconception that multiplication always makes things bigger.]

- *Ask students to create a pair of fractions to multiply to result in each situation:*
    - *the product is a bit less than $\frac{1}{2}$ [e.g., $\frac{9}{10} \times \frac{1}{2}$]*
    - *the product is very close to $\frac{3}{5}$ [e.g., $\frac{6}{5} \times \frac{3}{5}$]*
    - *the product is a bit more than $\frac{11}{10}$ [e.g., $\frac{6}{2} \times \frac{2}{5}$]*
- *Ask students to choose values for the blanks to make this true: $\frac{\square}{5} \times \frac{\square}{\square} = 1\frac{11}{15}$.*
- *Tell students that a recipe to serve 6 people requires $2\frac{2}{3}$ cups of sugar. Ask students to choose a number of people (other than 6) to decide how much sugar would be needed to make the adjusted recipe.*
- *Ask students to fill in the blanks as many ways as they can using fractions: $\frac{1}{12}$ is _____ of _____.*

Dividing with Fractions

Number and Operations—Fractions	CCSSM 5.NF

Apply and extend previous understandings of multiplication and division to multiply and divide fractions.

7. Apply and extend previous understandings of division to divide unit fractions by whole numbers and whole numbers by unit fractions.

   a. Interpret division of a unit fraction by a non-zero whole number, and compute such quotients. For example, create a story context for $\frac{1}{3} \div 4$, and use a visual fraction model to show the quotient. Use the relationship between multiplication and division to explain that $\frac{1}{3} \div 4 = \frac{1}{12}$ because $\frac{1}{12} \times 4 = \frac{1}{3}$.

   b. Interpret division of a whole number by a unit fraction, and compute such quotients. For example, create a story context for $4 \div \frac{1}{5}$, and use a visual fraction model to show the quotient. Use the relationship between multiplication and division to explain that $4 \div \frac{1}{5} = 20$ because $20 \times \frac{1}{5} = 4$.

   c. Solve real-world problems involving division of unit fractions by non-zero whole numbers and division of whole numbers by unit fractions, e.g., by using visual fraction models and equations to represent the problem. For example, how much chocolate will each person get if 3 people share $\frac{1}{2}$ lb of chocolate equally? How many $\frac{1}{3}$-cup servings are in 2 cups of raisins?

IMPORTANT UNDERLYING IDEAS

➤ *Dividing unit fractions by whole numbers.* Students are generally comfortable with the notion of sharing, so many of them are comfortable dividing a fraction by a whole number. Imagine, for example, that a winning raffle ticket provides the holder with $\frac{1}{5}$ of a certain prize, but 3 winners shared the cost of the ticket. The question is what fraction of the total prize each of the holders of the shared ticket gets. Students could calculate $\frac{1}{5} \div 3$ as the size of each share.

To get the exact amount, it would make sense to use a model. If students only divide up the first fifth in the diagram showing $\frac{1}{5}$, they cannot easily name the shaded part since the 7 parts are not of equal size.

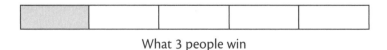

What 3 people win

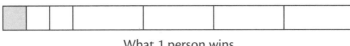

What 1 person wins

It would make sense, then, to divide each of the fifths, even those not being shared, to get equal parts; then students see that the amount of each share represents $\frac{1}{15}$ of the total.

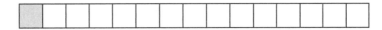

This makes sense since if each fifth is divided into 3 sections, there are 3×5 sections in total.

If they wished, students could check their answer, recognizing that whenever $a \div b = c$, then $b \times c = a$.

So, in the case of $\frac{1}{5} \div 3 = \frac{1}{15}$, $3 \times \frac{1}{15} = \frac{3}{15}$, or $\frac{1}{5}$, as is desired. More generally, if $\frac{1}{a}$ is shared by b people, each share is $\frac{1}{a \times b}$.

> **Dividing whole numbers by unit fractions.** Sometimes instead of a division problem involving sharing, the problem involves counting groups. For example, we might want to know how many $\frac{1}{3}$ cup scoops are needed to measure 2 cups of flour.

Students will realize that there are 3 scoops in each 1 cup. If 2 cups are required, then 2×3 scoops must be used. More generally, if counting the number of groups of $\frac{1}{b}$ in a, the result is $a \times b$ since there are a sets of b groups.

Good Questions to Ask

- *Ask students to create a model to show each of these:*

$$\frac{1}{8} \div 2 \qquad 2 \div \frac{1}{8}$$

- *Ask students whether $\frac{3}{5} \div 3$ or $3 \div \frac{3}{5}$ is greater and why their answer makes sense.*
- *Tell students that you divided a whole number by $\frac{1}{5}$. Ask them to name three possible answers and three impossible answers and explain each.* [Hopefully, students observe that the answer is always a multiple of 5.]
- *Ask students to create a problem that is solved by dividing 4 by $\frac{1}{4}$.*

Summary

The biggest hurdles for many Grade 5 students are an understanding of what decimal thousandths actually are, comfort with the relatively complicated processes of adding and subtracting fractions with different denominators, and not actually the performance of the multiplication algorithm for fractions but recognizing what situations call for multiplication and division of fractions.

Ironically, although the procedures for adding and subtracting fractions are more complex than those for multiplying and dividing, an understanding of when adding and subtracting is required in a problem situation is easier for most students to recognize than when multiplying or dividing is required.

Another critical idea at this level is a recognition of why the fraction sign is an implied division. Again, although this is easy to tell in a procedural way, it is harder for students to make sense of.

GRADE

Relating Fractions to Ratios

Ratios and Proportional Relationships	CCSSM 6.RP

Understand ratio concepts and use ratio reasoning to solve problems.

1. Understand the concept of a ratio and use ratio language to describe a ratio relationship between two quantities. For example, "The ratio of wings to beaks in the bird house at the zoo was 2:1, because for every 2 wings there was 1 beak." "For every vote candidate A received, candidate C received nearly three votes."

2. Understand the concept of a unit rate $\frac{a}{b}$ associated with a ratio $a{:}b$ with $b \neq 0$ and use rate language in the context of a ratio relationship. For example, "This recipe has a ratio of 3 cups of flour to 4 cups of sugar, so there is $\frac{3}{4}$ cup of flour for each cup of sugar." "We paid $75 for 15 hamburgers, which is a rate of $5 per hamburger."

3. Use ratio and rate reasoning to solve real-world and mathematical problems, e.g., by reasoning about tables of equivalent rates, tape diagrams, double number line diagrams, or equations.

> **Note.** There are other standards that are related to ratio and proportional reasoning found in the Common Core State Standards for Mathematics that are not addressed in this book. Here, the focus is only on the relationship between ratio/rate thinking and fractional thinking.

IMPORTANT UNDERLYING IDEAS

> **Associating fractions with ratios and rates.** Ratio situations always involve a comparison of two or more quantities. But there are also fractions associated with any ratio.

For example, the ratio of dark circles to white ones is 4:3.

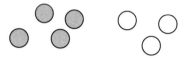

There are many fractions that may be associated with this comparison.

- $\frac{4}{7}$ describes the fraction of all circles that are dark. (a part-to-whole ratio)
- $\frac{3}{7}$ describes the fraction of all circles that are white. (a part-to-whole ratio)
- $\frac{7}{4}$ describes how many times as many circles there are than dark circles.
- $\frac{7}{3}$ describes how many times as many circles there are than white circles.
- $\frac{4}{3}$ compares the number of dark circles to white ones. If the number of white circles is known, it is multiplied by $\frac{4}{3}$ to determine the number of dark ones. (a part-to-part ratio)
- $\frac{3}{4}$ compares the number of white circles to dark ones. If the number of dark circles is known, it is multiplied by $\frac{3}{4}$ to determine the number of white ones. (a part-to-part ratio)

Recognizing these different viewpoints is an opportunity to use the mathematical practice standard of looking for and making use of structure.

Rates can also be related to fractions. If, for example, 2 boxes of an item cost $12, then the equivalent fractions to $\frac{12}{2}$ of $\frac{6}{1}$, $\frac{18}{3}$, $\frac{48}{8}$, etc. help one determine the costs for 1, 3, and 8 boxes. The equivalent fractions to $\frac{2}{12}$ of $\frac{1}{6}$, $\frac{3}{18}$, $\frac{8}{48}$, etc. help one determine the number of boxes that can be purchased for $6, $18, $48, etc. Part-to-part ratios are not as meaningful in a rate situation.

The concept of unit rate is also related to fraction division, as described earlier.

> **The notion of equivalence.** Just as a fraction can be renamed to an equivalent form by multiplying numerator and denominator by a non-zero amount, so can a ratio or rate. For example, the fraction $\frac{3}{5}$ is equivalent to the fraction $\frac{6}{10}$; similarly, when there are 3 circles for every 5 squares, there are 6 circles for every 10 squares, so the ratios 3:5 and 6:10 are equivalent. Or if 5 boxes cost $3, then 10 boxes cost $6, so the rates 5 for $3 and 10 for $6 are equivalent.

Understanding equivalence is fundamental for solving ratio, rate, or percent problems. Solving any such problem always involves determining an equivalent rate or ratio to a given one. For example, determining the number of boys in a class if the ratio of boys to girls is 6:5 and there are 10 girls in the class is a question of renaming 6:5 to an equivalent ratio where the second term is 10 (instead of 5).

Determining the distance traveled in 8 hours at a speed of 48 mph is a question of determining an equivalent to $\frac{48}{1}$ of the form $\frac{\square}{8}$. Determining what the original price of an item is if 75% of the price is $24 is a question of determining an equivalent ratio to $\frac{75}{100}$ of the form $\frac{24}{\square}$.

> **The distinction between fractions and ratios and rates.** Clark, Berenson, and Cavey (2003) explore how different people see fractions as a subset of ratios, ratios as a subset of fractions, ratios as identical to fractions, and ratios as totally different from fractions.

Although fractions and ratios are linked, as described in the section above, there are distinctions. They both compare two amounts. In the case of the ratio or rate, it is the terms of the ratio (or rate) that are compared, and in the case of fractions, it is a comparison of the numerator and denominator. On the other hand, whereas a fraction is a single number associated with one point on a number line, a ratio or rate might not be viewed as a single number.

Why this distinction is important is that "operating" with fractions is handled differently than operating with ratios. We add fractions by combining two parts of the same whole. For example, $\frac{2}{3} + \frac{1}{4}$ is the length of a segment that goes from 0 to $\frac{1}{4}$ appended to a segment that goes from 0 to $\frac{2}{3}$; both are related to the same unit, 1. We do not add numerators and denominators to determine the total length. On the other hand, it makes sense to say that, if there are 2 circles for every 3 squares in one set and 1 circle for every 4 squares in another, then if the sets are combined there are 3 circles for every 7 squares; in this case, we add first terms and second terms.

Good Questions to Ask

- *Ask students to draw any number of dark and light squares and write a number of different fractions associated with the comparison.*
- *Ask students to draw light and dark squares so that each of the fractions $\frac{3}{5}$ and $\frac{5}{8}$ could describe the situation. Then ask what other fractions also describe the situation.*
- *Ask students to represent a ratio situation where the first quantity is much less than one fourth of the second one. Then ask what they notice about the fractions that describe that situation.* [They might notice that the fraction comparing the first quantity to the second is less than $\frac{1}{4}$, the quantity comparing the second quantity to the first is more than $\frac{4}{1}$, the quantity comparing the first quantity to the total is less than $\frac{1}{5}$, etc.]
- *Ask students to use a model to show why the ratio 5:8 can also be viewed as the equivalent ratio 15:24.*

Dividing Fractions by Fractions

The Number System	CCSSM 6.NS

> *Apply and extend previous understandings of multiplication and division to divide fractions by fractions.*

1. Interpret and compute quotients of fractions, and solve word problems involving division of fractions by fractions, e.g., by using visual fraction models and equations to represent the problem. For example, create a story context for $\frac{2}{3} \div \frac{3}{4}$ and use a visual fraction model to show the quotient; use the relationship between multiplication and division to explain that $\frac{2}{3} \div \frac{3}{4} = \frac{8}{9}$ because $\frac{3}{4}$ of $\frac{8}{9}$ is $\frac{2}{3}$. (In general, $\frac{a}{b} \div \frac{c}{d} = \frac{ad}{bc}$.) How much chocolate will each person get if 3 people share $\frac{1}{2}$ lb of chocolate equally? How many $\frac{3}{4}$-cup servings are in $\frac{2}{3}$ of a cup of yogurt? How wide is a rectangular strip of land with length $\frac{3}{4}$ mi and area $\frac{1}{2}$ square mi?

IMPORTANT UNDERLYING IDEAS

> ➤ *Meanings of division involving two fractions.* When working with whole numbers, students used a number of different meanings for division.

- 12 ÷ 3 could describe how many groups of 3 are in 12.
- 12 ÷ 3 could mean "What number do I multiply by 3 to get 12?"
- 12 ÷ 3 could describe the length of a rectangle with area 12 square units and width of 3 units
- 12 ÷ 3 could describe the size of a share if 3 people equally share 12 items.

This last meaning can also be used to describe a unit rate (e.g., how much does 1 package cost if 3 packages cost $12).

Division by a fraction can continue to be used to determine how many groups. For example, $\frac{1}{2} \div \frac{1}{3}$ is calculated to decide how many times to fill a $\frac{1}{3}$ cup scoop to measure out $\frac{1}{2}$ cup of something.

Division by a fraction can continue to be used to refer to what number to multiply by. For example, $\frac{3}{5} \div \frac{1}{3}$ asks what to multiply $\frac{1}{3}$ by to get $\frac{3}{5}$. The context might be to determine the scale factor that is used on a diagram that changes a line of $\frac{1}{3}$ of a unit to $\frac{3}{5}$ of a unit.

Division by a fraction can continue to be used to determine the length of a rectangle when the area and the width are known. For example, $\frac{12}{5} \div \frac{2}{3}$ could describe the length of a rectangle with area $\frac{12}{5}$ square units and width $\frac{2}{3}$ of a unit.

But it does not feel right to think of $\frac{3}{5} \div \frac{2}{3}$ as sharing $\frac{3}{5}$ among $\frac{2}{3}$, since we usually talk about sharing into a whole-number of groups. It does make sense to think about unit rate, an alternate "sharing" meaning, when dividing by a fraction. For example, $\frac{3}{5} \div \frac{2}{3}$ can be used to solve this problem: If you fill $\frac{3}{5}$ of a container in $\frac{2}{3}$ of an hour, how much or how many containers would you fill in 1 hour (the unit rate)? To solve the problem, students could draw a model like this.

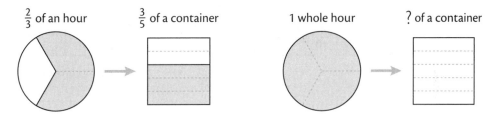

They could notice that if $\frac{3}{5}$ of a container is filled in $\frac{2}{3}$ of an hour, half that amount $(\frac{3}{10})$ could be filled in the other $\frac{1}{3}$ of the hour.

So the unit rate (or the amount filled in an hour) is $\frac{3}{5} + \frac{3}{10} = \frac{9}{10}$ of a container that could be filled in the whole hour. And, indeed, $\frac{3}{5} \div \frac{2}{3} = \frac{9}{10}$. This is an example of the mathematical practice standard of reasoning abstracting and quantitatively.

> ***Beginning with the concrete.*** Focusing on the "counting how many groups" meaning of division, students can use pattern blocks or fraction strips to model division calculations. For example, to model $\frac{1}{2} \div \frac{1}{6}$ (which asks how many $\frac{1}{6}$s are in $\frac{1}{2}$), students could use pattern blocks. If the blocks are named as shown:

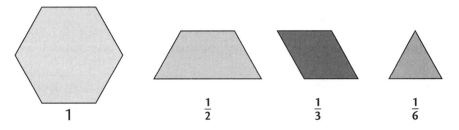

then $\frac{1}{2} \div \frac{1}{6}$ asks how many triangles fit on the trapezoid, so $\frac{1}{2} \div \frac{1}{6} = 3$.

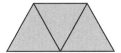

Or $\frac{1}{2} \div \frac{1}{3}$ asks how many parallelograms fit on the trapezoid, so $\frac{1}{2} \div \frac{1}{3} = 1\frac{1}{2}$ (or $\frac{3}{2}$).

Fraction strips can also be used to show why $\frac{3}{5} \div \frac{5}{10} = \frac{6}{5}$ (or $1\frac{1}{5}$)

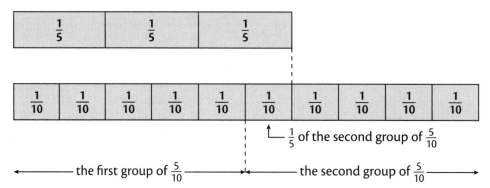

Some students will think the answer is $1\frac{1}{10}$ rather than $1\frac{1}{5}$ since there is a $\frac{1}{10}$ piece left over after the first $\frac{5}{10}$ is fit in. But students need to be reminded that we are counting the number of groups of $\frac{5}{10}$, so it is a full group and another $\frac{1}{5}$ of a group (even though it's $\frac{1}{10}$ of a whole).

Fraction strips can also explain why $\frac{4}{10} \div \frac{1}{2} = \frac{4}{5}$ since $\frac{4}{5}$ of a $\frac{1}{2}$ fits in $\frac{4}{10}$.

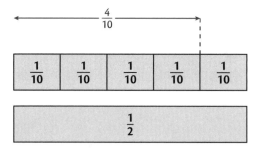

➤ **Using common denominators as a division strategy.** Thinking of division as counting groups can support the advantage of using what is called the common denominator algorithm. Equivalent fractions with common denominators are determined for the fractions being divided. The answer is the quotient of the two numerators. For example, to determine $\frac{2}{3} \div \frac{3}{4}$, the equivalent fractions $\frac{8}{12}$ and $\frac{9}{12}$ are used. Since 8 twelfths is $\frac{8}{9}$ of 9 twelfths, only $\frac{8}{9}$ of a $\frac{9}{12}$ fits into $\frac{8}{12}$ and the quotient of the two fractions is $\frac{8}{9}$.

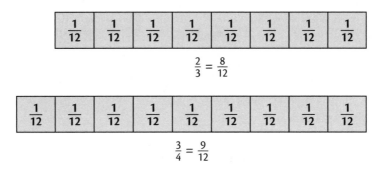

$$\frac{2}{3} = \frac{8}{12}$$

$$\frac{3}{4} = \frac{9}{12}$$

Similarly, $\frac{1}{3} \div \frac{1}{10} = \frac{10}{30} \div \frac{3}{30} = \frac{10}{3}$ or $3\frac{1}{3}$. That means there are $3\frac{1}{3}$ sets of $\frac{1}{10}$ in $\frac{1}{3}$.

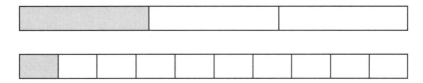

becomes

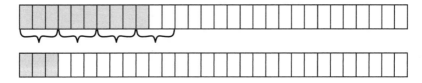

Using common denominators is a way to use the same units. The question that was originally asking how many $\frac{1}{10}$s are in $\frac{1}{3}$ becomes a question asking how many $\frac{3}{30}$ are in $\frac{10}{30}$, which is really asking how many groups of 3 fit in 10. The critical piece was getting the same units.

➤ *Multiplying by the reciprocal as a division strategy.* To explain the more traditional reciprocal, or invert and multiply, strategy, it is useful to use either the inverse multiplication or the unit rate meaning of division.

To solve, for example, $\frac{2}{3} \div \frac{3}{5}$, a student is looking for what to multiply $\frac{3}{5}$ by to get $\frac{2}{3}$.

$$\frac{3}{5} \times \frac{\square}{\square} = \frac{2}{3}.$$

The student could be led to see that multiplying $\frac{3}{5}$ by $\frac{5}{3}$ results in 1, so multiplying $\frac{3}{5}$ by $\frac{5}{3}$ followed by $\frac{2}{3}$, or $\frac{3}{5} \times \frac{5}{3} \times \frac{2}{3}$, leads to $\frac{2}{3}$.

$$\frac{3}{5} \times \frac{5}{3} \times \frac{2}{3} = \frac{15}{15} \times \frac{2}{3}$$
$$= 1 \times \frac{2}{3}$$

Using the unit rate concept, imagine that someone has filled $\frac{2}{3}$ of a container in $\frac{5}{4}$ of an hour and we want to know how much was filled in an hour. One would first divide $\frac{2}{3}$ by 5 to figure out how much was done in $\frac{1}{4}$ of an hour. Multiplying that amount by 4 would allow us to determine the amount in 1 hour.

The operations were $\frac{2}{3} \div 5 \times 4$. This is identical to taking $\frac{1}{5}$ of $\frac{2}{3}$ and multiplying by 4 or multiplying $\frac{2}{3} \times \frac{4}{5}$.

➤ **Estimating quotients of fractions.** Students should be encouraged to estimate quotients before calculating. When initially presented a division question, they can start by deciding whether the quotient is more or less than 1.

For example, $\frac{9}{10} \div \frac{1}{3}$ is more than 1 since $\frac{1}{3}$ is less than $\frac{9}{10}$, so at least one group of $\frac{1}{3}$ fits in $\frac{9}{10}$. However, $\frac{3}{5} \div \frac{7}{8}$ is less than 1 since $\frac{3}{5}$ is not as big as $\frac{7}{8}$, so a whole $\frac{7}{8}$ will not fit into a $\frac{3}{5}$.

Students might estimate more closely as well. For example, for $\frac{2}{3} \div \frac{1}{4}$, the student realizes that $\frac{2}{3} \div \frac{1}{3} = 2$. But $\frac{1}{4}$ is less than $\frac{1}{3}$, so more $\frac{1}{4}$s will fit in $\frac{2}{3}$ than $\frac{1}{3}$s fit in $\frac{2}{3}$; the quotient is more than 2, but less than 3 ($\frac{3}{4} \div \frac{1}{4}$).

For $\frac{9}{8} \div \frac{3}{7}$, the student realizes this is more than $1 \div \frac{1}{2}$, or 2, since we are fitting pieces smaller than $\frac{1}{2}$ into a piece bigger than 1.

When dividing mixed numbers, students might rename them as improper fractions to determine an exact answer, but leave them in mixed number form to estimate.

For example, $2\frac{4}{5} \div 1\frac{1}{2}$ should be about 2 since this is about $3 \div 1\frac{1}{2}$. The exact answer is $\frac{14}{5} \div \frac{3}{2}$, which is $\frac{28}{15}$, or $1\frac{13}{15}$.

Good Questions to Ask

- *Provide models such as these and ask students what division or divisions each shows. [It might be $\frac{5}{8} \div \frac{2}{5}$ in the first case and $\frac{2}{3} \div \frac{5}{12}$ in the second.]*

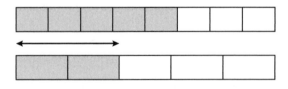

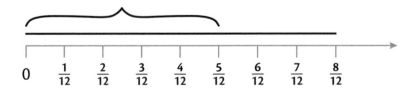

- *Early on, provide a fraction tower, such as the one below. Ask students to find two fractions where the smaller fraction fits into the larger one a little more than 2 times. This is actually asking what two fractions can be divided so that the quotient is slightly more than 2. [Possibilities include $\frac{1}{5}$ and $\frac{1}{2}$, $\frac{1}{3}$ and $\frac{1}{8}$, $\frac{2}{3}$ and $\frac{1}{4}$, etc.]*

1																			

The fraction tower shows rows of:
- $\frac{1}{2}$, $\frac{1}{2}$
- $\frac{1}{3}$, $\frac{1}{3}$, $\frac{1}{3}$
- $\frac{1}{4}$, $\frac{1}{4}$, $\frac{1}{4}$, $\frac{1}{4}$
- $\frac{1}{5}$ (×5)
- $\frac{1}{6}$ (×6)
- $\frac{1}{8}$ (×8)
- $\frac{1}{9}$ (×9)
- $\frac{1}{10}$ (×10)
- $\frac{1}{12}$ (×12)
- $\frac{1}{15}$ (×15)
- $\frac{1}{18}$ (×18)
- $\frac{1}{20}$ (×20)

- Ask students to compare $\frac{5}{6} \div \frac{2}{3}$ and $\frac{2}{3} \div \frac{5}{6}$. Do the same with $\frac{3}{8} \div \frac{2}{9}$ and $\frac{2}{9} \div \frac{3}{8}$. And then again $\frac{5}{3} \div \frac{2}{7}$ and $\frac{2}{7} \div \frac{5}{3}$. Then ask students to try to explain what happened. [They should notice that the results are "reciprocals" (i.e., if one is $\frac{a}{b}$, the other is $\frac{b}{a}$). This makes sense. For example, if there are $\frac{5}{4}$ of a $\frac{2}{3}$ in $\frac{5}{6}$, that means that the $\frac{2}{3}$ must be $\frac{4}{5}$ of the $\frac{5}{6}$, the reciprocal.]

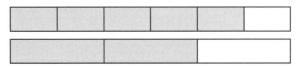

This is an example of the mathematical practice standard of looking for and making use of structure.

Nyack College Library

- Ask unit rate problems such as: If you can drive $\frac{2}{9}$ of the way to somewhere in $\frac{3}{5}$ of an hour, how much of the way can you drive in an hour?
- Have students use the digits 4, 9, 3, and 5 to create as great and as small an answer as possible in the following expression:

$$\frac{\square}{\square} \div \frac{\square}{\square}$$

- Ask students to create a story problem that is solved by calculating $\frac{4}{5} \div \frac{2}{3}$.

Interpreting Rational Numbers

The Number System	CCSM 6.NS

Apply and extend previous understandings of numbers to the system of rational numbers.

5. Understand that positive and negative numbers are used together to describe quantities having opposite directions or values (e.g., temperature above/below zero, elevation above/below sea level, credits/debits, positive/negative electric charge); use positive and negative numbers to represent quantities in real-world contexts, explaining the meaning of 0 in each situation.

6. Understand a rational number as a point on the number line. Extend number line diagrams and coordinate axes familiar from previous grades to represent points on the line and in the plane with negative number coordinates.

   a. Recognize opposite signs of numbers as indicating locations on opposite sides of 0 on the number line; recognize that the opposite of the opposite of a number is the number itself, e.g., $-(-3) = 3$, and that 0 is its own opposite.

   c. Find and position integers and other rational numbers on a horizontal or vertical number line diagram; find and position pairs of integers and other rational numbers on a coordinate plane.

7. Understand ordering and absolute value of rational numbers.

   a. Interpret statements of inequality as statements about the relative position of two numbers on a number line diagram. For example, interpret $-3 > -7$ as a statement that -3 is located to the right of -7 on a number line oriented from left to right.

   b. Write, interpret, and explain statements of order for rational numbers in real-world contexts. For example, write $-3°C > -7°C$ to express the fact that $-3°C$ is warmer than $-7°C$.

IMPORTANT UNDERLYING IDEAS

➤ *Meaning of negative rational numbers.* Students are normally introduced to negative integers before they work with negative rational numbers. By this time, the concept that $-\frac{2}{3}$ is the opposite of $\frac{2}{3}$, that is, the number placed on a number line a distance of $\frac{2}{3}$ of a unit from 0 to its left, will make sense.

There are fewer everyday situations where students use negative rational numbers as compared to positive ones, but some examples are temperatures or elevations above or below sea level.

If students know how to place positive fractions on a number line, they can place a negative rational number $-\frac{a}{b}$ either by:

- locating its opposite, $\frac{a}{b}$, and then determining the mirror image on the other side of 0 on the number line, or
- locating $-a$ on the number line, dividing the segment from $-a$ to 0 into b partitions, and using the left end point of the partition closest to 0 to represent $-\frac{a}{b}$, or
- dividing the segment from -1 to 0 into b partitions and counting back a of those partitions from 0.

For example, to locate $-\frac{3}{5}$, one can show any of the following:

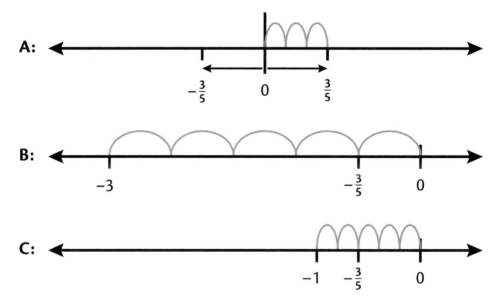

> **Renaming negative rational numbers.** Students also need to realize that $-\frac{2}{3}$, $\frac{-2}{3}$, and $\frac{2}{-3}$ are all names for the same point. One way to do this is to think about the fractions as division.

- $-\frac{2}{3}$ is the opposite of the result when dividing 2 by 3.
- $\frac{-2}{3}$ is the result when dividing -2 by 3. Sharing -2 among 3 people is the opposite of sharing $+2$ among 3 people. So $\frac{-2}{3} = -\frac{2}{3}$.
- $\frac{2}{-3}$ can be written as an equivalent fraction if we multiply the numerator and denominator by the same amount. If we multiply the numerator and

denominator by –1, we get an equivalent fraction, but it's $\frac{-2}{3}$, which was already established as the same as $-\frac{2}{3}$.

➤ *Comparing and ordering rational numbers.* Students should realize that, like all other numbers on the number line, numbers farther to the left are less and those farther to the right are more. Once students know how to place negative rational numbers on the number line, they should be able to order them.

Students should recognize that:

- any positive rational number is greater than any negative rational number, since it is farther to the right on the number line
- the order of two negative rational numbers is the opposite of the order of their opposites (e.g., $-\frac{6}{4} < -\frac{1}{2}$ since $\frac{1}{2} < \frac{6}{4}$ [again because of relative positions on the number line])

Good Questions to Ask

- *Ask students for a number just a little bit less than $-\frac{3}{4}$.*
- *Ask students to choose digits for the blanks and order the rational numbers from least to greatest, explaining their thinking.*

$$\frac{-\square}{\square} \qquad \frac{-3}{\square} \qquad -\frac{5}{\square} \qquad \frac{\square}{-3} \qquad -\frac{\square}{6}$$

- *Ask students for different ways to locate $-\frac{7}{5}$ on a number line. Discuss whether renaming the fraction as a mixed number is useful and why.*
- *Ask students to fill in negative rational values to make these true:*

    _____ *is almost as close to $-\frac{3}{4}$ as it is to –2.*
    _____ *is about twice as far from $-\frac{7}{8}$ as it is from –2.*
    _____ *is about $\frac{1}{3}$ as far from 3 as it is from $-\frac{8}{5}$.*

Summary

The new concepts related to fractions that students must master in Grade 6 involve division of fractions, the relationship between ratio and fractions, and the use of "negative fractions" or rational numbers. Many students, however, are still likely to require more experience with the fraction operation foundations that are a focus of Grade 5.

GRADE 7

Ratios and Proportional Relationships

Ratios and Proportional Relationships	CCSM 7.RP
Analyze proportional relationships and use them to solve real-world and mathematical problems.	

1. Compute unit rates associated with ratios of fractions, including ratios of lengths, areas, and other quantities measured in like or different units. For example, if a person walks $\frac{1}{2}$ mile in each $\frac{1}{4}$ hour, compute the unit rate as the complex fraction $\frac{\frac{1}{2}}{\frac{1}{4}}$ miles per hour, equivalently 2 miles per hour.
3. Use proportional relationships to solve multistep ratio and percent problems. *Examples:* simple interest, tax, markups and markdowns, gratuities and commissions, fees, percent increase and decrease, percent error.

> **Note:** There are other standards that are related to ratio and proportional reasoning found in the Common Core State Standards for Mathematics that are not addressed in this book. Here, the focus is only on the relationship between ratio/rate thinking and fractional thinking.

IMPORTANT UNDERLYING IDEAS

> **Unit rates.** A unit rate tells how many units of one quantity are associated with one unit of another. It could, for example, be miles driven per 1 hour or dollars spent per 1 item or number of doughnuts per 1 box. An understanding of the notion of unit rate is critical to student success in work with linear relations in Grades 7 and 8.

For example, determining the algebraic description of the relationship between total cost and total months as a gym member described by the table of values below requires a recognition that there is a unit rate of $20 per month associated with a gym membership.

Number of Months	Total Membership Cost
0	$100
1	$120
2	$140
3	$160
4	$180

The concepts required to work effectively with unit rates are built on rational number understanding. Realizing that a rate of $20 for 3 books is the same rate as a unit rate of $6.67 for one book is based on a recognition that the fractions $\frac{20}{3}$ and $\frac{6\frac{2}{3}}{1}$ comparing the number of dollars to the number of books are equivalent.

Deciding whether two variables are proportional involves an ability to recognize equivalent ratios, but that is built on recognizing equivalent fractions.

When unit rates are determined to compare two quantities, there is usually more than one way to do it that makes sense. For example, if a car drives 45 miles in 50 minutes, unit rates of $\frac{0.9 \text{ miles}}{1 \text{ minute}}$ and $\frac{54 \text{ miles}}{1 \text{ hour}}$ both describe the situation. In addition, the unit rate of $\frac{1.11 \text{ minutes}}{1 \text{ mile}}$ also makes sense. This tells how many minutes you need to drive a single mile instead of how many miles you can drive in a minute (or an hour).

➤ **Complex fractions.** Conventionally, students meet only fractions where the numerator and denominator are integers. But, in fact, numbers of the form $\frac{a}{b}$ where a and b are fractions, called complex, or compound, fractions, are also meaningful. This might occur in a situation where, for example, a student rewrites a rate of 117 miles in 2 hours as the unit rate of $58\frac{1}{2}$ miles in 1 hour, i.e., $\frac{58\frac{1}{2}}{1}$.

For example, $\frac{2\frac{1}{2}}{5}$ is legitimately another way to describe the fraction $\frac{1}{2}$. This is because it can be rewritten as the quotient of two integers where the numerator is half of the denominator. Students can visualize this as a whole divided into 5 equal parts where $2\frac{1}{2}$ parts are used.

This also makes sense because students have learned that fractions represent implied division. If we divide $2\frac{1}{2}$ by 5, we are determining how many 5s fit into $2\frac{1}{2}$, which is clearly $\frac{1}{2}$ of a 5. Fractions can appear in either the numerator or the denominator of a complex fraction, or both.

> *Relating the solving of proportions to fraction knowledge.* When solving percent, rate, or ratio problems, students can benefit by using their fraction knowledge in many different ways.

One valuable piece of fraction knowledge is an understanding of equivalence. To solve any percent, ratio, or rate problem, we are generally looking for an equivalent form of a given rate, ratio, or percent. For example, if a map scale has the ratio 1:20,000 and we want to know how far apart two places really are that are $2\frac{1}{2}"$ apart on a map, we are essentially looking for a fraction equivalent to $\frac{1}{20,000}$ with a numerator of $2\frac{1}{2}$.

If we knew that we could tile $2\frac{1}{2}$ rooms in $\frac{3}{5}$ of a day, and we were trying to figure out how many rooms we could tile in a full day, we could either think about an equivalent fraction to $\frac{2\frac{1}{2}}{\frac{3}{5}}$ with a denominator of 1, or we could think of dividing $2\frac{1}{2}$ by $\frac{3}{5}$.

If we were trying to figure out how many boys and girls would be in a class if the ratio of boys:girls is 3:5 and the total number of students is 24, students could use fraction multiplication, multiplying $24 \times \frac{3}{8}$ to determine the number of boys and $24 \times \frac{5}{8}$ to determine the number of girls.

Once students begin to formally solve proportions using cross-multiplication, they are, in essence, renaming both ratios using equivalent fractions with a common denominator and then writing an equation that sets the numerators equal. For example: $\frac{3}{7} = \frac{x}{10}$ is solved by writing $\frac{3}{7}$ as $\frac{30}{70}$ and $\frac{x}{10}$ as $\frac{7x}{70}$. Setting the numerators as equals results in the equation $30 = 7x$ (the result of cross-multiplying).

Good Questions to Ask

- Ask students to solve the following problem: *Suppose a container of laundry detergent costs $42 for 100 oz. Write two unit rates, one describing how much money 1 oz costs and one describing how much detergent you can get for $1. Which unit rate do you think is more useful? Why?* [Note that the rates $\frac{\$0.42}{1\ oz}$ and $\frac{2.38\ oz}{\$1}$ seem quite different to many students. The latter is more unfamiliar, but students should be encouraged to consider its potential usefulness.]

- Ask students to create several complex fractions that would be equivalent to $\frac{2}{3}$. [Possibilities include $\frac{1}{1\frac{1}{2}}$, $\frac{3}{4\frac{1}{2}}$, and $\frac{\frac{1}{2}}{\frac{1}{4}}$.]

- Have students consider the fractions $\frac{2\frac{1}{2}}{3\frac{1}{2}}$ compared to $\frac{2}{3}$ and $\frac{3}{4}$, $\frac{3\frac{1}{2}}{4\frac{1}{2}}$ compared to $\frac{3}{4}$ and $\frac{4}{5}$, and $\frac{4\frac{1}{2}}{5\frac{1}{2}}$ compared to $\frac{4}{5}$ and $\frac{5}{6}$.

  Have them describe what they notice and argue as to why what they see makes sense. [Each time the complex fraction will be between the two simple fractions given. Notice that each time the numerator is halfway between the given simple fractions, and the same holds true for the denominator.]

- Ask students to create a ratio problem that might be solved by dividing $\frac{2}{3}$ by $\frac{3}{8}$. This focuses students on the mathematical practice standard of modeling with mathematics.

- Ask students to describe a rate problem that is solved by multiplying by $\frac{3}{8}$.

Adding and Subtracting Rational Numbers

The Number System	CCSSM 7.NS
Apply and extend previous understandings of operations with fractions to add, subtract, multiply, and divide rational numbers.	

1. Apply and extend previous understandings of addition and subtraction to add and subtract rational numbers; represent addition and subtraction on a horizontal or vertical number line diagram.

   a. Describe situations in which opposite quantities combine to make 0. For example, a hydrogen atom has 0 charge because its two constituents are oppositely charged.

   b. Understand $p + q$ as the number located a distance $|q|$ from p, in the positive or negative direction depending on whether q is positive or negative. Show that a number and its opposite have a sum of 0 (are additive inverses). Interpret sums of rational numbers by describing real-world contexts.

   c. Understand subtraction of rational numbers as adding the additive inverse, $p - q = p + (-q)$. Show that the distance between two rational numbers on the number line is the absolute value of their difference, and apply this principle in real-world contexts.

   d. Apply properties of operations as strategies to add and subtract rational numbers.

IMPORTANT UNDERLYING IDEAS

> *The zero principle.* Initially students work with integers and then extend their understanding to rational numbers to realize that any rational number added to its opposite yields 0. $-1 + 1 = 0$ since -1 is defined to be the number 1 less than 0, so adding 1 results in a sum of 0.

For the same reasons, any negative integer added to its opposite is 0. For example, -3 is 3 below 0, so adding 3 brings it back up to 0. It feels reasonable to most students that the same would be true with any rational number.

One might argue, for example, that if $-\frac{2}{3}$ is $\frac{2}{3}$ of a unit below 0, then adding $\frac{2}{3}$ brings us back to 0. This can be supported using visuals, although many students will be able to reason abstractly.

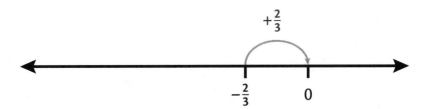

➤ **Meaning of addition of rational numbers.** As with whole numbers and positive fractions, adding always involves combining. Just as $\frac{2}{5} + \frac{3}{5}$ can be modeled on a number line by starting at 0, moving $\frac{2}{5}$ of a unit forward and then $\frac{3}{5}$ of another unit forward, $-\frac{2}{5} + \frac{3}{5}$ suggests starting at $-\frac{2}{5}$ and moving $\frac{3}{5}$ of a unit forward.

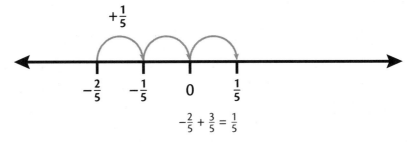

The result is $(-2 + 3)$ fifths, or $\frac{1}{5}$.

Adding a negative involves moving backward, so $\frac{3}{5} + (-\frac{2}{5})$, which should have the same result as $-\frac{2}{5} + \frac{3}{5}$ is modeled as below and the result is the same.

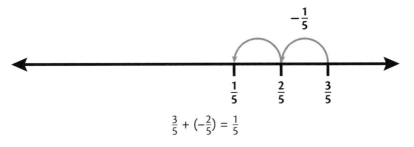

In general, the sum of $\frac{a}{b}$ and $\frac{c}{b}$ is $(a + c)$ copies of $\frac{1}{b}$, or $\frac{a+c}{b}$. If the rational numbers have different denominators, they can be renamed as equivalents with a common denominator.

Based on what they learned with integers, students should realize that:

- adding two negative rational numbers results in a negative rational even farther back from 0. For example, $-\frac{4}{5} + (-\frac{2}{3})$ results in $-(\frac{4}{5} + \frac{2}{3})$ or $-0.8 + -0.667 = -1.4667$.

- adding two positive rational numbers results in a positive rational number
- adding a negative rational number far away from 0 to a positive rational number closer to 0 results in a negative rational number closer to 0 than the original negative rational number (e.g., $-\frac{4}{5} + \frac{1}{5} = -\frac{3}{5}$ or $-0.8 + 0.2 = -0.6$)
- adding a negative rational number close to 0 to a positive rational number farther from 0 results in a positive rational number closer to 0 than the original positive rational number (e.g., $-\frac{1}{5} + \frac{4}{5} = \frac{3}{5}$ or $-0.2 + 0.8 = 0.6$)

➤ *Meaning of subtraction of rational numbers.* For many students, subtraction means taking away, but taking away a negative amount is a bit awkward and can be confusing. Some students simply rationalize that taking away "bad" is "good," but this is not a real explanation. It is important that students understand why taking away a negative is adding the opposite. It is also important that they know when a different approach than taking away might actually be more efficient.

One way to explain why we add the opposite is to look at subtraction not as take-away but as the opposite of addition. $a - b = c$ if c is the amount to add to b to get a.

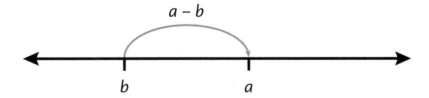

For example, $3 = 5 - 2$, since we add 3 to 2 to get to 5.

With this in mind, $\frac{5}{4} - (-\frac{2}{4}) = \frac{5}{4} + \frac{2}{4}$, since we have to add $\frac{5}{4} + \frac{2}{4}$ to $-\frac{2}{4}$ to get to $\frac{5}{4}$.

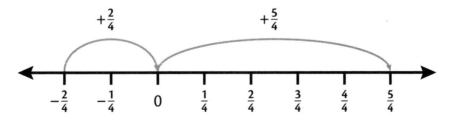

$\frac{2}{4}$ is the distance from $-\frac{2}{4}$ to 0 and $\frac{5}{4}$ is the rest of what must be added to get to $\frac{5}{4}$.

Notice that it is appropriate to *start* with the number *after* the minus sign, since that it what is added to in order to get the first number. To calculate $(-\frac{5}{3}) - (-\frac{2}{3})$, a student might draw the picture below and note that we have to add $-\frac{3}{3}$, to get from $-\frac{2}{3}$ to $-\frac{5}{3}$,

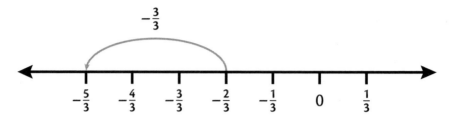

It is not as obvious that we are adding $\frac{2}{3}$ to $-\frac{5}{3}$, but it can be shown by combining a $-\frac{5}{3}$ amount with a $+\frac{2}{3}$ amount as below. What is left of the $-\frac{5}{3}$ amount is exactly the distance shown above. This is an example of the mathematical practice standard of constructing viable arguments.

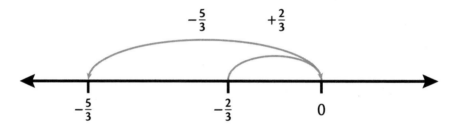

Another approach to subtracting rational numbers is based on recognizing that, if two numbers are a certain distance apart, then the same amount can be added to both numbers to preserve that distance.

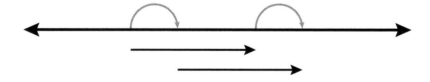

Students are familiar with this concept using whole numbers, where they might solve 14 – 9 by changing the question to 15 – 10, moving each number 1 forward on the number line. Using this idea, (–4.2) – (–3.1) must have the same difference as [(–4.2) + (3.1)] – [(–3.1) + (3.1)]. The amount 3.1 is added to make the second number 0. Since 0 has no effect when subtracting, the student sees that (–4.2) – (–3.1) = (–4.2) + (3.1).

A more algebraic approach can also be used, although it is usually not as convincing for students as the visual interpretations presented above. A student could think:

If I want to add an amount to $-\frac{2}{3}$ to get to $-\frac{5}{3}$, I could do it in steps.
First I add $\frac{2}{3}$ to $-\frac{2}{3}$ (its opposite) in order to get to 0.
Then I add the $-\frac{5}{3}$, since $0 + (-\frac{5}{3}) = -\frac{5}{3}$.
So $-\frac{5}{3} - (-\frac{2}{3}) = \frac{2}{3} + (-\frac{5}{3})$.

More generally, to figure out the number to add to $-b$ to get to a, we could think of first adding b to get to 0 and then adding a. So $a - (-b) = b + a$ (or $a + b$).

Another algebraic approach is to work with equations:

If $a - (-b) = c$, then add $-b$ to both sides of the equation.
$a - (-b) + (-b) = c + (-b)$.

On the left, the expression is $a - 0$, since subtracting a number $(-b)$ and then adding it back yields 0. Therefore, $a = c + (-b)$.

Adding $+b$ to both sides of the equation leads to $a + b = c + (-b) + b$.

On the right, if we add $-b$ and b, we get 0, so the right-hand expression is actually c, which was $a - (-b)$.

This is an example of the mathematical practice standard of looking for and making use of structure.

We can also think about subtraction as take-away. Having a positive rational and taking away a smaller one makes sense. Having a negative rational and taking away a greater negative rational (a value closer to 0) makes sense. For example, we can think of $-\frac{3}{5} - (-\frac{1}{5})$ as beginning with 3 jumps of $-\frac{1}{5}$ from 0 and removing 1 of those jumps of $-\frac{1}{5}$, leaving 2 of them. So the answer is 2 jumps of $-\frac{1}{5}$ from 0, or $-\frac{2}{5}$. Take-away is a less comfortable approach if negatives are taken from positives or positives from negatives.

> **Strategies for adding and subtracting rational numbers.** Students combine what they know about adding and subtracting fractions with what they know about adding and subtracting integers, in order to master adding and subtracting rational numbers. Ideas for adding and subtracting positive fractions can be found in the Grade 4 section.

For example, in order to add $-\frac{2}{3} + \frac{5}{7}$, students first decide whether $\frac{5}{7}$ or $-\frac{2}{3}$ is farther from 0 by comparing $\frac{5}{7}$ and $\frac{2}{3}$. Once they realize that the fraction $\frac{5}{7}$ is greater than the fraction $\frac{2}{3}$, they realize that the sum is positive. To find the distance from 0, we subtract $\frac{2}{3}$ from $\frac{5}{7}$ to get the final result of $\frac{1}{21}$.

But to add $-\frac{3}{8} + (-\frac{4}{3})$, students realize that the result must be negative and the distance from 0 is $\frac{3}{8} + \frac{4}{3}$, or $\frac{41}{24}$, so the result is $-\frac{41}{24}$.

Students can use the same strategies for adding and subtracting mixed numbers as they did with fractions, keeping in mind the issues of signs discussed in the sections above.

Good Questions to Ask

- Ask students: *You subtract two fractions and the result can be written as the decimal −4.2. What could the fractions be? How do you know there are many possible solutions?* [Students should realize that once they have one solution, they need only add the same amount to both numbers to get many more solutions.]
- Ask students how to tell whether $\frac{a}{b} + (-\frac{c}{d})$ *is positive or negative, assuming* a, b, c, *and* d *are positive, without actually calculating the result.*
- Ask students how they would explain each of these:
  - *why* $(-\frac{2}{3}) - (-\frac{3}{4}) = -\frac{2}{3} + \frac{3}{4}$
  - *why* $(-\frac{2}{3}) + (-\frac{3}{4})$ *is the opposite of* $(\frac{2}{3} + \frac{3}{4})$
  - *why* $\frac{2}{3} - \frac{3}{4}$ *is the opposite of* $\frac{3}{4} - \frac{2}{3}$

Multiplying and Dividing Rational Numbers

The Number System	CCSSM 7.NS

Apply and extend previous understandings of operations with fractions to add, subtract, multiply, and divide rational numbers.

2. Apply and extend previous understandings of multiplication and division and of fractions to multiply and divide rational numbers.

   a. Understand that multiplication is extended from fractions to rational numbers by requiring that operations continue to satisfy the properties of operations, particularly the distributive property, leading to products such as $(-1)(-1) = 1$ and the rules for multiplying signed numbers. Interpret products of rational numbers by describing real-world contexts.

   b. Understand that integers can be divided, provided that the divisor is not zero, and every quotient of integers (with non-zero divisor) is a rational number. If p and q are integers, then $-\frac{p}{q} = \frac{-p}{q} = \frac{p}{-q}$. Interpret quotients of rational numbers by describing real-world contexts.

   c. Apply properties of operations as strategies to multiply and divide rational numbers.

IMPORTANT UNDERLYING IDEAS

> *Meanings of multiplication and division of rational numbers.* Although a number of former meanings of multiplication and division continue to apply when rational numbers are negative, some do not. For example, it makes little sense to talk about multiplication as the area of a rectangle with a negative length or width. But partitioning, scaling, and the notion of relative size still apply.

　　It also makes little sense to talk about division to determine the length of a rectangle since areas and widths cannot be negative. But sharing, unit rates, counting how many groups, and viewing division as inverse multiplication still apply. In addition, the use of patterns to make sense of sign laws become useful. Details of these ideas appear in the next two sections.

> *Multiplying rational numbers.* One can think about multiplying a positive by a negative in terms of partitioning and relative size. For example, $\frac{4}{5} \times (-\frac{2}{3})$ can be interpreted as measuring $\frac{4}{5}$ of the distance from 0 to $-\frac{2}{3}$.

From work with fractions, students know that $\frac{4}{5}$ of $\frac{2}{3}$ is $\frac{8}{15}$, so the landing point after the fourth jump must be $-\frac{8}{15}$; it's on the negative side of 0. They might also recognize that since $-\frac{2}{3} = -\frac{10}{15}$, each jump back from 0 is $-\frac{2}{15}$, which means that 4 of the jumps end at $-\frac{8}{15}$.

Although the commutative principle holds, so that $-\frac{2}{3} \times \frac{4}{5}$ has to be equal to $\frac{4}{5} \times -\frac{2}{3}$, there is some value in interpreting a negative multiplied by a positive in its own right. One possibility relates to dilatations and scale. It makes sense to talk about $-\frac{2}{3}$ of $\frac{4}{5}$ from the point of view of scale if the negative sign is interpreted as changing direction (as per a dilatation). So $-\frac{2}{3}$ of $\frac{4}{5}$ might involve going in the opposite direction $\frac{2}{3}$ of the way from the center of dilatation, as shown below.

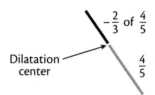

$-\frac{2}{3} \times \frac{4}{5}$ might also be interpreted in terms of distance and time. One might think of 2×45 as indicating where someone will be, relative to that person's current position, in 2 hours of traveling at 45 mph. It would make sense, then, to interpret -2×45 as where the person was 2 hours ago, relative to the current position. Similarly, if you think of $\frac{4}{5}$ as a speed (e.g., $\frac{4}{5}$ miles per minute), then $-\frac{2}{3} \times \frac{4}{5}$ describes where the person was $\frac{2}{3}$ of a minute ago relative to the person's current position. The answer of $-\frac{8}{15}$ means that the person was $\frac{8}{15}$ of a mile behind where he or she currently is. This is an example of the practice standard of modeling with mathematics.

Multiplying negatives by negatives is harder to make sense of without quite contrived explanations. But the notion can be explained algebraically. For example, let's consider the above example. Since opposites add to 0, $\frac{2}{3} + (-\frac{2}{3}) = 0$. Both sides of the equation can be multiplied by $-\frac{4}{5}$, so

$$[\tfrac{2}{3} \times (-\tfrac{4}{5})] + [(-\tfrac{2}{3}) \times (-\tfrac{4}{5})] = 0$$

Since $\frac{2}{3} \times (-\frac{4}{5}) = -\frac{8}{15}$, and since opposites add to 0, it must be true that $-\frac{2}{3} \times (-\frac{4}{5})$ is the opposite of $-\frac{8}{15}$, or $\frac{8}{15}$.

Another approach to multiplying two negatives to get a positive is based on patterns. Students can look, for example, at this pattern to help see why $-\frac{1}{2} \times (-\frac{1}{2})$ must be $+\frac{1}{4}$.

$$2 \times (-\tfrac{1}{2}) = -1$$
$$\tfrac{3}{2} \times (-\tfrac{1}{2}) = -\tfrac{3}{4}$$
$$1 \times (-\tfrac{1}{2}) = -\tfrac{1}{2}$$
$$\tfrac{1}{2} \times (-\tfrac{1}{2}) = -\tfrac{1}{4}$$
$$0 \times (-\tfrac{1}{2}) = 0$$
$$-\tfrac{1}{2} \times (-\tfrac{1}{2}) = ?$$

Since the product keeps increasing by $\frac{1}{4}$ as the left-hand factor decreases by $\frac{1}{2}$, it only make sense that the missing value be $+\frac{1}{4}$. This is an example of the mathematical practice standard of looking for and expressing regularity in repeated reasoning.

➤ *Dividing rational numbers.* One can always think about division as inverse multiplication. Since a negative multiplied by a positive is negative, it has to be true that a negative divided by a negative is positive, a positive divided by a negative is negative, and a negative divided by a positive is negative.

$$\text{If } -a \times (+b) = -c, \text{ then}$$
$$-c \div (-a) = +b \text{ and}$$
$$-c \div (+b) = -a$$

Sharing can be used to make sense of dividing by a positive whole number, and unit rate for dividing by a positive fraction (as explained in the Grade 6 section). For example, $-0.4 \div 4$ is the share size if a debt of 0.4 units is shared among 4 people; each share is negative since it is part of a debt. $-\frac{2}{3} \div \frac{1}{5}$ can be interpreted as the unit rate if $\frac{2}{3}$ of a container is emptied in $\frac{1}{5}$ of an hour, and there is interest in how many containers could be emptied in an hour (assuming no loss of time switching between containers).

The counting-how-many-groups approach can be used to make sense of dividing a negative by a negative. For example, $-\frac{3}{5} \div (-\frac{1}{5})$ asks how many jumps of $-\frac{1}{5}$ from 0 would make a distance of $-\frac{3}{5}$. The result is +3, since it is 3 jumps. This is true even if the result is not a whole number; for example, $-\frac{3}{4} \div (-\frac{1}{2}) = \frac{3}{2}$ since it takes $\frac{3}{2}$ of a jump of size $-\frac{1}{2}$ to reach $-\frac{3}{4}$ from 0.

The most difficult situation to explain without resorting to the relationship with multiplication is dividing a negative by a positive. One could think about scale.

Using scale, $\frac{3}{5} \div (-\frac{1}{5})$ describes the nature of the dilatation that would change a distance of $\frac{1}{5}$ to a distance of $\frac{3}{5}$ in the opposite direction. Since it is the opposite direction, the sign is negative and clearly the distance was tripled, so the result is −3.

Good Questions to Ask

- *Suggest to students that you multiplied a rational number by another rational number and that the result was just a bit closer to 0 than the number you began with, but on the other side of 0. Ask for several possible pairs of rational numbers.*
- *Ask students to create a visual explanation to show why each is true:*
  - $-\frac{4}{3} \times (\frac{3}{8}) = -\frac{1}{2}$
  - $\frac{5}{6} \times (-\frac{4}{5}) = -\frac{4}{6}$
  - $(-\frac{4}{5}) \div (\frac{1}{3}) = -\frac{12}{5}$
  - $(-\frac{4}{5}) \div (-\frac{6}{5}) = \frac{4}{6}$
- *Ask students to describe a situation that might lead someone to divide −3.2 by 4.*
- *Ask students to create an argument for why $-\frac{2}{3} \times (-3) = 2$ without just using a rule.*

Writing Rational Numbers as Decimals

The Number System	CCSSM 7.NS
Apply and extend previous understandings of operations with fractions to add, subtract, multiply, and divide rational numbers.	

2. Apply and extend previous understandings of multiplication and division and of fractions to multiply and divide rational numbers.
   d. Convert a rational number to a decimal using long division; know that the decimal form of a rational number terminates in 0s or eventually repeats.

IMPORTANT UNDERLYING IDEAS

> *Categorizing decimals as repeating or terminating.* The terms *terminating* and *repeating decimals* are unfamiliar to many students. In some sense the term *terminating* is misleading, since even terminating decimals can be made to seem repeating by using more 0s. For example, 0.23 is terminating, but can be written as 0.2300000 . . .

However, students do need to understand that a terminating decimal is one that can be written exactly as tenths, hundredths, thousandths, ten thousandths, etc. (i.e., as a whole number of units that are the reciprocal of a positive power of 10). This means that, if desired, terminating decimals can be written with a finite number of digits.

The decimal 0.21212121 . . . is clearly repeating, but the decimal 0.4212121 . . . , which is partially repeating (i.e., repeating after the digit 4), is still regarded as a repeating decimal.

Students at this level rarely encounter nonrepeating decimals that do not terminate, even though they do exist.

> *Converting rational numbers to repeating decimals.* Because students have learned that $\frac{a}{b} = a \div b$, they can convert rational numbers expressed as fractions into decimals. In so doing, they will notice that the decimals always either terminate or repeat, but it will not be obvious as to why without analysis.

Students might be encouraged to use equivalent fractions with denominators that are powers of 10 when it is possible. For example, $\frac{3}{40}$ can be rewritten as $\frac{75}{1000}$, or 0.075. But sometimes this is not possible. In fact, if the denominator of the fraction, when written in simplest form, has factors other than 2 or 5, numbers which are factors of 10, it will not be possible to rewrite that fraction as an equivalent fraction with a whole number numerator and a denominator of 10, 100, etc. For example, $\frac{2}{3}$ cannot be written as a whole number of tenths or hundredths or thousandths or ten thousandths . . . , because the 3 cannot be multiplied by any whole number in order to make this happen.

We teach students that fractions are implied division and that, in order to determine the decimal equivalent for a fraction, we divide the numerator by the denominator. But writing $\frac{2}{3}$ as $2 \div 3$ does not really help determine the decimal; it is writing $\frac{2}{3}$ as 20 tenths $\div$ 3 or 200 hundredths $\div$ 3 or 2000 thousandths $\div$ 3 that actually helps us determine the decimal.

Writing $\frac{2}{3}$ as 20 tenths yields the tenths place in the decimal, 6 tenths. Since the result is not exact, the student might reconsider $\frac{2}{3}$ as 200 hundredths. Now not only does the student realize that the tenths place is 6, but so is the hundredths place. At this point students might notice that the number of units left is 2 each time, so the same thing will happen over and over. It's at this point that the student realizes that the decimal repeats. $3\overline{)2.0}^{\,0.6}$ with a remainder of 2 tenths becomes $3\overline{)2.00}^{\,0.66}$ with a remainder of 2 hundredths, and perhaps $3\overline{)2.000}^{\,0.666}$ with a remainder of 2 thousandths.

If students use a calculator, the repetition will be clear right away, but thinking in the way shown above helps students understand where the decimal came from.

Sometimes the repetition is not immediate. For example, writing $\frac{1}{6}$ as a decimal begins by writing it as 10 tenths, resulting in a tenths digit of 1:

$$6\overline{)1.0}^{\,0.1} \text{ with a remainder of 4 tenths}$$

Then the student might rewrite 1 as 100 hundredths to get the hundredths digit:

$$6\overline{)1.00}^{\,0.16} \text{ with a remainder of 4 hundredths.}$$

Now that the remainder is the same, the student may realize that he or she is back to the same situation and the decimal will repeat.

Other times, students might completely lose faith in the repetition since it takes so long. For example, $\frac{1}{17}$ does not repeat for 17 digits, and it will not be obvious with a typical calculator that only shows 8 or 10 digits when the repetition actually begins. Although students can learn how to determine all the digits, as will be explained below, it is important for them to understand that if they divide by 17, there are only 16 possible remainders, so eventually a remainder will repeat and the decimal in the quotient will have to repeat. In other words, the number of digits in a repetition will always be less than the denominator, since the only possible remainders when dividing by 17 are 1, 2, 3, . . . 15, 16.

To determine all the digits for $\frac{1}{17}$, students can use a calculator to learn the first group of digits (0.058823529). The student could then multiply 0.05882352 (ignoring the last digit in case it was rounded up) by 17 to see that it is short of 1 by $\frac{16}{100,000,000}$. Then that 16 hundred millionths could be divided by 17 to get 0.9411764705 hundred millionths. Noticing the 05 again, the student realizes the digits are finally repeating, so $\frac{1}{17}$ = 0.05882362941176470588236294117647 . . .

There are no real-world applications student would encounter that would require this sort of precision, so the only purpose in doing this is to convince the student that the decimal, which should repeat, actually does.

Good Questions to Ask

- *Ask students how they might convince someone that the decimal for $\frac{5}{8}$ has to be terminating and the one for $\frac{5}{12}$ has to be repeating, even before calculating the decimals.* [Students should recognize that 1000 is a multiple of 8, but no power of 10 is a multiple of 12. This is an example of asking students to utilize the mathematical practice standard of constructing viable arguments.]
- *Ask students how they would explain to someone why the decimal for $\frac{5}{6}$ has to repeat.* [Hopefully, students will realize that the only remainders possible when dividing into any number of 10s, 100s, 1000s, etc. are 1, 2, 3, 4, and 5, and once a remainder repeats, the decimal will repeat.]
- *Ask students when $\frac{\square}{6}$ might be written as a terminating decimal.* [Students need to realize that the numerator would have to be a multiple of 3.]

Summary

Although there is not a lot of new content in Grade 7 work with fractions, there is the introduction of repeating decimals in more formal ways and attention to work with operations involving negatives, as well as a more formal focus on proportionality. The repeating decimal relationship is mathematically interesting, although it is not highly related to further learning. On the other hand, competence with fractional operations and an understanding of principles of proportionality are critical for student success in later grades in math.

CONCLUSION

MANY TEACHERS were simply never taught a lot of the ideas to which they could expose their students that would really help them develop a better grasp of fraction concepts. I hope that this resource provides some of that valuable mathematical background to the classroom teacher working with fraction instruction.

The Good Questions provided in this resource are only samples, but what should be noticed is that most of them foster higher-level thinking and evoke the mathematical practice standards that are critical in today's math classroom. The more teachers can get their students to not just find solutions but to really *think* about mathematical ideas, the better off the students will be. The sample questions provided here almost all require students to think about the math, not just do it.

BIBLIOGRAPHY

Ball, D. L. (1993). Halves, pieces, and twoths: Constructing representational contexts in teaching fractions. In T. Carpenter, E. Fennema, & T. Romberg (Eds.), *Rational numbers: An integration of research* (pp. 157–196). Hillsdale, NJ: Erlbaum.

Barnett-Clarke, C., Fisher, W., Marks, R., & Ross, S. (2010). *Developing essential understanding of rational numbers for teaching mathematics in Grades 3–5.* Reston, VA: National Council of Teachers of Mathematics.

Behr, M., Harel ,G., Post T., & Lesh R. (1993). Rational numbers: Toward a semantic analysis—Emphasis on the operator construct. In T. Carpenter, E. Fennema, & T. Romberg (Eds.), *Rational numbers: An integration of research* (pp. 13–47). Hillsdale, NJ: Lawrence Erlbaum Associates.

Charalambous, C. Y., & Pitta-Pantazi, D. (2005). Revising a theoretical model on fraction implications for teaching and research. *Proceedings of the 29th Conference of the International Group for the Psychology of Mathematics Education, 2,* 233–240. Available at www.emis.de/proceedings/PME29/PME29CompleteProc/PME29Vol2Adl_Fre.pdf

Clark, M. R., Berenson, S. B., & Cavey, L. O. (2003). A comparison of ratios and fractions and their roles as tools in proportional reasoning. *Journal of Mathematical Behavior, 22,* 297–317.

Clarke, D. (2006). Fractions as division: The forgotten notion? *Australian Primary Mathematics Classroom, 11*(3), 4–10.

Cramer, K., Wyberg, T., & Leavitt, S. (2008). The role of representations in fraction addition and subtraction. *Mathematics Teaching in the Middle School, 13,* 490–496.

Empson, S. (1995). Using shared situations to help children learn fractions. *Teaching Children Mathematics, 2,* 110–114.

Empson, S., & Levi, L. (2011). *Extending children's mathematics: Fractions and decimals.* Portsmouth, NH: Heinemann.

Empson, S., Levi, L., & Carpenter, T. (2010). The algebraic nature of fractions: Developing relational thinking in elementary school. Available at http://mishtadim.files.wordpress.com/2011/04/algebraic-nature-of-fractions-empson.pdf

Hecht, S. A., & Vagi, K. J. (2010). Sources of group and individual differences in emerging fraction skills. *Journal of Educational Psychology, 102,* 843–859.

Hecht, S. A., Vagi, K. J., & Torgesen, J. K. (2007). Fractions and proportional reasoning. In D. B. Berch, & M. M. Mazzocco (Eds.), *Why is math so hard for some children? The nature and origins of mathematical learning difficulties and disabilities* (pp. 121–132). New York: Brookes Publishing.

Kamii, C., & Clark, F. B. (1995). Equivalent fractions: Their difficulty and educational implications. *Journal of Mathematical Behavior, 14,* 365–378.

Kieran, T. E. (Ed.). (1980). *Recent research on number learning.* Eric Clearinghouse for Science, Mathematics and Environmental Education, Columbus, Ohio. ED 212 463.

Kieran, T. E. (1988). Personal knowledge of rational numbers: Its intuitive and formal development. In J. Hiebert & M. Behr (Eds.), *Number concepts and operations in the middle grades* (pp. 162–181). Reston, VA: National Council of Teachers of Mathematics.

Lamon, S. J. (2006). *Teaching fractions and ratios for understanding: Essential content knowledge and instructional strategies for teachers.* New York: Routledge.

Mack, N. K. (1995). Confounding whole-number and fraction concepts when building on informal knowledge. *Journal for Research in Mathematics Education, 26,* 422–441.

McNamara, J., & Shaughnessy, M. M. (2010). *Beyond pizzas and pies: 10 essential strategies for supporting fraction sense, Grades 3–5.* Sausalito, CA: Math Solutions Publications.

McNamara, J., & Shaughnessy, M. M. (2011). Student errors: What they can tell us about what students DO understand? Available http://www.mathsolutions.com/documents/StudentErrors_JM_MS_Article.pdf

Moss, J., & Case, R. (1999). Developing children's understanding of the rational numbers: A new model and an experimental curriculum. *Journal for Research in Mathematics Education, 30,* 122–147.

National Council of Teachers of Mathematics. (2000). *Principles and standards for school mathematics.* Reston, VA: National Council of Teachers of Mathematics.

National Mathematics Advisory Panel. (2008). *Foundations for success; The final report of the national mathematics advisory panel.* Washington, DC: U.S. Department of Education.

National Research Council. (2001). *Adding it up: Helping children learn mathematics* (J. Kilpatrick, J. Swafford, & B. Findell, Eds.). Mathematics Learning Study Committee, Center for Education, Division of Behavioral and Social Science and Education. Washington, DC: National Academy Press.

Noura, K. (2009, December). Understanding fractions: What happens between kindergarten and the army? Paper presented at the annual conference of The Mathematical Association of Victoria, Victoria, Australia.

Petit, M. M., Laird, R. E., & Marsden, E. L. (2010). *A focus on fractions: Bringing research to the classroom.* New York: Routledge.

Pitkethly, A., & Hunting, R. P. (1996). A review of recent research in the area of initial fraction concepts. *Educational Studies in Mathematics, 30,* 5–38.

Siegler, R. S., Carpenter, T., Fennell, F., Geary, D., Lewis, J., Okamoto, Y., Thompson, L., & Wray, J. (2010). *Developing effective fractions instruction for kindergarten through 8th grade: A practice guide* (NCEE #2010-4039). Washington, DC: National Center for Education Evaluation and Regional Assistance, Institute of Education Sciences, U.S. Department of Education. Available at www.whatworks.ed.gov/publications/practice guides

Siegler, R. S., Fazio, L. K., Bailey, D. H., & Zhou, X. (2013). Fractions: The new frontier for theories of numerical development. *Trends in Cognitive Sciences, 17,* 13–19.

Small, M. (2005). *PRIME: Numbers and operations.* Toronto: Thomson Nelson.

Small, M. (2013). *Making math meaningful to Canadian students* (2nd ed.). Toronto: Nelson Education Ltd.

Stafylidou, S., & Vosniadou, S. (2004). The development of students' understanding of the numerical value of fractions. *Learning and Instruction, 14,* 503–518.

Streefland, L. (1993). Fractions: A realistic approach. In T. P. Carpenter, E. Fennema, & T. A. Romberg (Eds.), *Rational numbers: An integration of research* (pp. 289–326). Mahwah, NJ: Lawrence Erlbaum Associates.

Teaching and Learning Research Programme. (2006). Teaching and Learning Research Briefing 13: Fractions: Difficult but crucial in mathematics learning. Available at www.tlrp.org/pub/documents/no13_nunes.pdf

Watanabe, T. (2002). Representations in teaching and learning fractions. *Teaching Children Mathematics, 8,* 457–463.

Watanabe, T. (2006). The teaching and learning of fractions: A Japanese perspective. *Teaching Children Mathematics, 12,* 368–374.

Index

INDEX OF SUBJECTS AND CITED AUTHORS

INDEX OF COMMON CORE STANDARDS IN MATHEMATICS

The Number System

Apply and extend previous understandings of multiplication and division to divide fractions by fractions.
  Grade 6, 94–100

Apply and extend previous understandings of numbers to the system of rational numbers.
  Grade 6, 101–103

Apply and extend previous understandings of operations with fractions to add, subtract, multiply, and divide rational numbers.
  Grade 7, 109–114, 115–118, 119–121

ABOUT THE AUTHOR

MARIAN SMALL is the former Dean of Education at the University of New Brunswick. She speaks regularly about differentiating instruction and asking better questions in K–12 mathematics.

She has been an author on many mathematics text series at both the elementary and the secondary levels. She has served on the author team for the National Council of Teachers of Mathematics (NCTM) Navigation series (pre-K–2), as the NCTM representative on the Mathcounts question writing committee for middle-school mathematics competitions throughout the United States, and as a member of the editorial panel for the NCTM 2011 yearbook on motivation and disposition.

Dr. Small is probably best known for her books *Good Questions: Great Ways to Differentiate Mathematics Instruction* and *More Good Questions: Great Ways to Differentiate Secondary Mathematics Instruction* (with Amy Lin). *Eyes on Math: A Visual Approach to Teaching Math Concepts* was published in 2013. She is also author of the second edition of a text for university pre-service teachers and practicing teachers, *Making Math Meaningful to Canadian Students: K–8*, as well as the professional resources *Big Ideas from Dr. Small: Grades 4–8*; *Big Ideas from Dr. Small: Grades K–3*; and *Leaps and Bounds toward Math Understanding: Grades 3–4, Grades 5–6*, and *Grades 7–8*, all published by Nelson Education Ltd.

She led the research resulting in the creation of maps describing student mathematical development in each of the five NCTM mathematical strands for the K–8 levels and has created the associated professional development program, PRIME.

8376002

DATE DUE
